The Home Studio Guide to Microphones

by Loren Alldrin

*Technical Edit by George Petersen
and Michael Molenda*

6400 Hollis Street
Emeryville, CA 94608

06 05 04 03 02 01 00 99 98 97   6 5 4 3 2 1

Library of Congress Catalog Card Number: 97-073716

Book design, layout, and cover art: Linda Gough

Cover photograph: Susana Millman

Illustrations: Loren Alldrin

Technical editors: George Petersen, Michael Molenda

Production staff
Mike Lawson: publisher, Lisa Duran: editor, Randy Antin: editorial assistant, Don Washington: operations coordinator,
Teresa Poss: administrative assistant, Ellen Richman: production director, Sherry Bloom: production assistant

6400 Hollis Street
Emeryville, CA 94608
(510) 653-3307

Also from MixBooks:
Anatomy of a Home Studio
The AudioPro Home Recording Course, Volumes 1 and 2
I Hate the Man Who Runs This Bar!
How to Make Money Scoring Soundtracks and Jingles
The Art of Mixing: A Visual Guide to Recording, Engineering, and Production
500 Songwriting Ideas (For Brave and Passionate People)
Music Publishing: The Real Road to Music Business Success, Rev. and Exp. 4th Ed.
How to Run a Recording Session
Mix Reference Disc, Deluxe Ed.
The Songwriters Guide to Collaboration, Rev. and Exp. 2nd Ed.
Critical Listening and Auditory Perception
Keyfax Omnibus Edition
Modular Digital Multitracks: The Power User's Guide
Concert Sound
Sound for Picture
Music Producers
Live Sound Reinforcement

Also from EMBooks:
Making the Ultimate Demo
Tech Terms: A Practical Dictionary for Audio and Music Production
Making Music With Your Computer

Printed in Auburn Hills, Michigan

ISBN 0-918371-22-8

For Mackenzie

Contents

113

SECTION SIX: MICROPHONE BUYER'S GUIDE

151

APPENDIX A:
MICROPHONE SOUND TROUBLESHOOTER

154

APPENDIX B:
MICROPHONE MANUFACTURERS

156

GLOSSARY

162

SUGGESTED READING

163

INDEX

Acknowledgments

I'd like to thank Mike Lawson, Lisa Duran and the whole MixBooks staff for a job well done; and Ken Reichel (Audio-Technica), Mark Gilbert (Shure Bros.), Gene Lawson (Lawson Inc.), Wes Dooley (Audio Engineering Associates), Rick Frank (Shure Bros.) and David Josephson (Josephson Engineering) for their valuable insights into microphone design. Special thanks go to my wife, Kristen Alldrin, whose help, encouragement and patience made this book possible. Ultimate thanks go to the Creator of music itself.

Introduction

Welcome to *The Home Studio Guide to Microphones*. The fact that you're reading this says several things about you. First, you're one of those rare people who reads introductions. Good for you. Authors sometimes make their most profound statements in the first few pages of their books.

Second, you've got a hunch that the mic you choose—and where you put it—has a significant effect on the quality of your recordings. This places you in even rarer company than being a reader of book introductions.

Let's face it, half the fun of owning a studio is learning about, buying and using gear. Many of us count the days until our next big purchase, rating the quality of our studios by the number of blinking lights and LCD displays they have. "If I could just buy that new Yamalexinger octal-tasking multiprocessor," the reasoning so often goes, "my recordings will sound just like the pros." Manufacturers are happy to feed this kind of thinking, spending huge sums of money to convince you that great recordings are no further away than your next gear purchase.

While certain pieces of outboard gear do perform amazing feats of sound processing, they're rarely the key to a great recording. Instead, a great recording is the result of the right mic capturing a great performance.

Sound simple? It is.

It's no exaggeration to say that the transducer (the device that converts one form of energy into another) is the most important link in any signal chain. For us recording folk, that transducer is the microphone. No other component in your studio will have as great an effect on the recorded sound as the mic, be it tube preamp, compressor, EQ or digital processor. Likewise, no amount of after-the-fact processing will fully compensate for a poor transducer—excuse me— poor *microphone* choice.

This book has one simple goal: to help you make better choices and better recordings through an improved understanding of microphones. I'll begin by exploring the inner workings of microphones to see how they operate. Then, I'll cover specific techniques that will help you get the most out of your mics. Finally, I'll share information on dozens of microphones within the budget of most home studio owners.

I've made every effort to keep confusing technical jargon out of *The Home Studio Guide to Microphones*. Equations and formulas are fine for those with a background in electrical engineering, but they tend to confuse everyone else. This book focuses on what the average home studio recordist *really* needs to know to make better recordings.

As you read through this book, note how often words like "maybe," "some" and "usually" appear when describing mics. The use of such language underscores the fact that there are few absolutes in the realm of microphone performance. It's simply not possible that a given type of microphone will *always* sound a certain way, and people who say that they will are usually trying to sell you something.

This brings us around to the whole point of what we do: sound. As you press forward in your knowledge of microphones and recording techniques, remember that sound quality is entirely subjective. You are the one and only authority on what sounds right to *you*. In an industry where marketing departments craft their own flowery definitions of good sound, believe half of what you see and 7.2 percent of what you read.

Trust only what you hear.

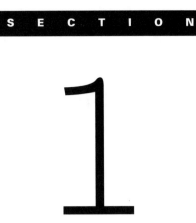

Microphone Technology

Though most mics look simple on the outside, there's a lot more going on inside than meets the eye. The microphone handles what may be the most crucial conversion in the whole recording process—from sound to electricity. Behind that innocent-looking grill, countless variables interact to determine the unique sound of each and every mic.

This section explores the inner workings of microphones to help you understand why a given mic or mic type performs the way it does. I'll start with a brief overview of how sound and electricity relate in the studio, then explain what makes common (and not-so-common) mic types tick, discuss mic pickup patterns and finish up with mic performance characteristics.

CHAPTER 1

Sounds and Signals

How some simple science can make for better recordings.

Any discussion of microphones would be incomplete without examining the basics of how sound works. So why read a chapter on the physics of sound in a book devoted to recording? The reason is simple: The better you understand the nature of sound, the more effectively you can capture it. Trial and error may allow you to create some good recordings, but a little knowledge can increase your chances of creating *great* recordings.

Let's start with a simple definition of sound. In its essence, sound is nothing more than tiny changes in air pressure. Like waves that radiate outward from a pebble thrown in a pond, sound moves out from its source in a pattern of high- and low-pressure areas. In the high-pressure zones (called compressions), air molecules are shoved together tighter than normal. In the low-pressure zones (rarefactions), air molecules are spaced out more than normal (see Figure 1.1).

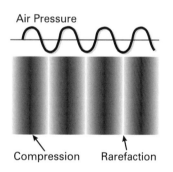

Figure 1.1. Sound is nothing more than alternating areas of high air pressure (compressions) and low air pressure (rarefactions).

These changes in air pressure cause small vibrations in our eardrums. Thanks to acoustic transmission, our eardrums "follow" the vibrations of the original sound source—be it a loudspeaker, string or drum head. Nerves carry the resulting impulses to the brain where we perceive them as sound.

The repeating high- and low-pressure zones of sound move past a given point at a speed we refer to as—you guessed it—the speed of sound. How many pressure changes pass a given spot in a certain period of time depends on the sound's *frequency*. If a sound has a high frequency (cymbal, triangle, dog whistle), the air pressure alternates from high to low very quickly. A high-frequency sound will cause a cycle from high to low and back again to occur many thousands of times per second. Low-frequency sounds (bass guitar, thunder, mechanical rumble) cause the sound pressure to alternate from high to low much more slowly, just a few dozen times per second (see Figure 1.2).

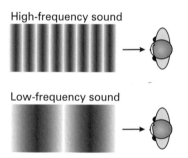

Figure 1.2. At higher sound frequencies, compressions and rarefactions are closer together than at low frequencies.

We measure a sound's frequency in cycles per second or "Hertz" (abbreviated "Hz"). If a sound causes 300 low-to-high pressure cycles to pass a given spot in one second, that sound has a frequency of 300Hz. The human ear can detect sounds from around 20Hz to 20kHz (20,000 cycles per second). This convenient approximation is optimistic; most people (especially men) can't hear past around 17kHz on the high end. As folks age, high-frequency hearing usually drops off markedly.

Related to frequency is a sound's *wavelength*. This measurement tells how far it is from one com-

2

pression (peak) or rarefaction (valley) to the next. Low-frequency sounds can have wavelengths of 40 feet or more, while the highest audible frequencies have wavelengths of roughly half an inch. Wavelength is inversely proportional to frequency: As frequency goes up, wavelength decreases (and vice versa). A 500Hz sound, for example, has a wavelength of about 2.26 feet. Double the frequency to 1,000Hz (or 1kHz), and wavelength is cut in half to 1.13 feet.

Every mic colors sound in its own unique way, which is something you can use to your advantage when recording.

Since we're most interested in sound as it relates to music, it's good to know how the ear responds to changes in frequency on a musical level. In simple terms, musical intervals are nothing more than mathematical relationships between frequencies. The most important interval to understand is the octave, which represents an even doubling (or halving) of frequency. Middle C on a piano, for example, sounds a note which has a frequency twice that of the C an octave below. Play the C an octave above middle C, and the frequency doubles. The even 2:1 ratio of the octave makes it a convenient measuring stick for quantifying the relationship between frequencies.

Though we often discuss a sound's frequency in the singular, most musical sounds consist of many frequencies. We call the lowest (and often loudest) frequency of a given sound the *fundamental*. This corresponds to the frequency of vibration of a string, reed, drum head, etc. Stacked above the fundamental are numerous *overtones* or *harmonics*, musical sounds that are related to the fundamental (see Figure 1.3). These overtones vary in frequency and volume from sound to sound and note to note and often extend well beyond the human hearing range.

Figure 1.3. Though a given instrument's fundamental pitches cover a relatively small frequency range, its overtones may extend beyond the limits of human hearing.

Though a musical sound's fundamental tells us the instrument's pitch, the overtones convey a sound's unique character. If a cello and a violin are playing the same note, they're both creating the same fundamental pitch. The overtones, however, are quite different, allowing us to distinguish one from the other. Overtones play a crucial role in defining the sound of all instruments, including the human voice.

How does this apply to choosing and using microphones? In a nutshell, the more evenly a mic responds to different frequencies, the more accurately it will capture the overtones of an instrument. A mic that doesn't offer an even frequency response will tend to emphasize certain overtones and suppress others. This changes the character of the recorded instrument, making it sound different on playback than it did when originally played. This coloration of the sound is not always a bad thing, as I'll explore in future chapters. Every mic colors sound in its own unique way, which is something you can use to your advantage when recording.

INTENSITY

Frequency measures the highness or lowness in pitch of a given sound; *sound pressure level* (SPL) defines how loud or intense the sound is. Our perception of how loud a sound is depends on how large the air pressure changes are, as this dictates the amount of movement of the eardrum.

The amount of energy carried by sound covers an incredibly broad range. A sound loud enough to cause pain, for example, carries roughly ten trillion times the energy of a sound that's barely audible. This makes quantifying sound pressure level on a linear scale very cumbersome (i.e., "Could you please turn the volume up about 35,800,000?"). To handle this broad range, we abandon the linear scale in favor of a logarithmic scale based on the bel, a unit of measure named after Alexander Graham Bell.

One bel represents a 10-fold increase in intensity, which tames our sound pressure level scale from 10,000,000,000,000 linear units to a more manageable 13 bels. The bel turns out to be a bit too coarse for most measurements, so we commonly measure sound and signal intensity in the decibel, or one-tenth of a bel. Measured in this finer logarithmic scale (abbreviated "dB"), our ears can discern a sound pressure level range of roughly 130dB SPL. It's relatively easy to remember that an increase of 10dB represents a 10-fold increase in sound pressure level, and an increase of 3dB causes a doubling of intensity.

This broad energy range provides a challenge for more than just our standards of measurement. At either extreme—quiet or loud—sound pressure levels can make the microphone's job a tough one. At their most quiet, sounds can disappear into ambient or electronic noise. At their loudest extreme, sounds can cause distortion by carrying more energy than the microphone can handle. With sounds at these extremes, mic selection becomes more critical. Very loud sounds require a mic capable of handling high sound pressure levels without distortion. Quiet sounds demand an extremely sensitive mic that generates very little noise of its own. I'll discuss maximum SPL and sensitivity figures further in Chapter 5.

Distance has a much greater effect on sound intensity than you may think. It seems logical that if you move to a new position twice as far from a given sound source, the resulting sound will be half as loud. In reality, a doubling of distance causes that sound's power to drop to ¼ of its original amount. Double the distance again and power will drop to ¹⁄₁₆ of its original amount. The same thing applies when moving a mic (or your ears) closer to the sound source. Cutting the distance in half doesn't just double the volume, it causes a fourfold increase in energy.

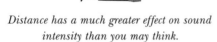

Distance has a much greater effect on sound intensity than you may think.

We call this phenomenon the "inverse square law." As sound leaves its source, the sound energy expands outward in a spherical shape. The energy is spread over the surface of this sphere, whose area increases in exponential fashion as it moves away from the source. A doubling of the sphere's radius, for example, stretches the sound energy over a surface with four times the original area (see Figure 1.4). We can express the inverse square law in this simplified equation:

$$\text{Intensity} = \frac{1}{(\text{change in distance}^2)}$$

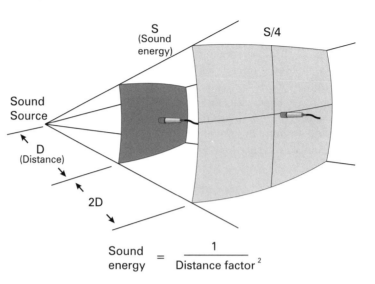

$$\frac{\text{Sound}}{\text{energy}} = \frac{1}{\text{Distance factor}^2}$$

Figure 1.4. Because sound energy radiates outward from its source in a spherical shape, a doubling of distance causes sound energy to drop to one-fourth. We call this the inverse square law.

PHASE

Phase describes the time relationship between two or more sounds, usually of identical frequency. When two identical sounds are in phase, their pressure energies combine and the result is a louder sound. When two sounds are out of phase, their energies subtract from each other, reducing or even eliminating the sound. Phase is worthy of your attention for one simple reason: Multiple sound waves or signals always interact with each other to some degree. Sometimes this interaction is constructive, other times it's destructive.

Multiple sound waves or signals always interact with each other to some degree.

Imagine that a microphone sits between two sound sources, each generating the same low-frequency sound at the same volume. If the mic picks up a high-pressure peak from both sources at the same time, the effective sound pressure is doubled and the mic puts out a stronger signal. These sounds are said to be "in phase." If one sound source's peak arrives at the same time as the other source's low-pressure zone, the two cancel each other out. These sounds are "out of phase," causing the mic to generate no low-frequency signal whatsoever (see Figure 1.5). Sounds can be partially out of phase as well, which causes varying degrees of reduction in signal strength.

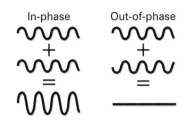

In-phase   Out-of-phase

Figure 1.5. When identical signals or sounds are in phase, their energies add. When they're out of phase, they cancel each other out.

When two sounds experience phase cancellation, all the sound doesn't simply disappear. Instead, the cancellation occurs only at those frequencies where there's a compression and rarefaction arriving at the same time. These "notches" appear at predictable frequencies throughout the audible spectrum, creating a frequency response that looks something like teeth on a comb. This is where the term "comb filter" comes from. Comparing Figure 1.6 to our ideal flat frequency response is visual proof that severe phase cancellation is a not a good way to achieve an uncolored recording.

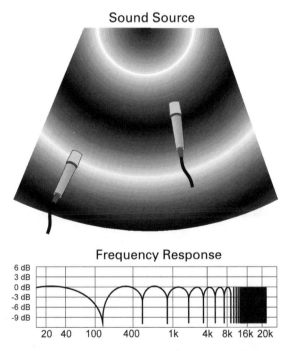

Sound Source

Frequency Response

Figure 1.6. When two mics sit at different distances from a sound source, the sound hits the mics at slightly different times. This time difference can cause phase cancellation at certain frequencies.

Because sound travels at the same speed at all locations, sound phase is a function of distance and time. If one sound travels further than another to reach the mic (hence taking longer to get there), certain frequencies will be out of phase. This can happen when one mic is picking up two or more different sound sources.

Phase cancellation also becomes a problem when multiple mics record the same sound source. When two or more mics are at different distances from a sound source, the sound doesn't arrive at the mics at the same instant (see Figure 1.6). When there's time delay, there's phase cancellation. This is why combining signals from multiple mics can cause a hollow, thin sound. I'll explore the 3:1 rule for minimizing phase cancellation in Chapter 8.

Finally, phase cancellation occurs when sound from a single source bounces off an object or wall and combines with sound hitting the mic directly (see Figure 1.7). In this case, the relative distances between the sound source, the mic and the reflective surface dictate the frequencies where phase cancellation occurs. Because high-frequency sounds cycle from high to low pressure over such a short distance, moving a mic as little as an inch can eliminate (or exaggerate) phase cancellation.

Sound Source

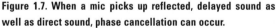

Figure 1.7. When a mic picks up reflected, delayed sound as well as direct sound, phase cancellation can occur.

It's interesting to note that phase cancellation has its benefits as well, especially in microphone design. Manufacturers make sound entering from the back of a microphone take a longer path than sound entering from the front to create a time delay and phase cancellation. This is one technique used to make a microphone more sensitive to sounds coming from directly in front of it.

When sound hits a solid surface, a certain amount of its energy is absorbed. What's left of the sound reflects off the surface and keeps going, often striking another surface and bouncing again. Sound continues to bounce around in enclosed spaces until its energy is completely dissipated. Depending on the mass and texture of the surfaces, different frequencies may bounce longer than others.

To the ear, caught in the crossfire of all this bouncing sound, these countless echoes blur into the smooth decay we call reverberation or ambience. Any sound we hear indoors is a blend of the direct sound and the delayed, reflected sound. If the mix of direct and reflected sounds contains more direct sound, we perceive that sound source as being closer to us. If the mix contains more reflected sound than direct sound, the source appears to be further away.

Like the ear, a microphone used in an enclosed space will pick up a blend of direct and reverberant sound. Controlling this blend is crucial to the recordist, because the amount of reverberant sound recorded plays a large role in where an instrument or voice "sits" in the mix. You can add artificial reverb to a sound after the fact, but it's almost impossible to remove excessive ambience from a recording.

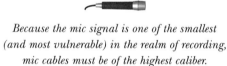

The amount of reverberant sound recorded
plays a large role in where an instrument or
voice sits in the mix.

We have two tools at our disposal for controlling the ratio of direct to reverberant sound: mic placement and mic directional pattern. The closer you place a mic to a sound source, the louder that source will be relative to the reflected sound. Place a mic on the other side of the room, and you may get more reverb than direct sound.

Nearly as effective as distance is the use of a directional mic. A directional mic, which is most sensitive to sounds coming from certain directions, will dramatically reduce the amount of reverberation recorded. It does this by rejecting reflected sounds that approach the mic from behind it or to the sides. A directional mic can be nearly twice as far from the sound source as a non-directional mic and pick up the same ratio of direct and reverberant sound.

Mic Signal Basics

With the basics of sound under our belts, let's explore some simple facts about microphone signals. A mic is just an expensive paperweight unless it's attached to something: Signal has to flow from mic to recorder or mixer. How you care for the precious microphone signal on this journey is very important. Improper mic cabling can compromise the sound of even the most expensive mic; proper cabling will ensure that you get the most out of any mic, regardless of cost.

All a signal needs to flow from point to point is a single piece of wire. In reality, though, such a simple cable wouldn't suffice. Our world is awash in stray signals, constantly emanating from all sorts of electronic equipment. Without some protection from this bombardment, the mic signal would pick up untold amounts of electronic noise. Because the mic signal is one of the smallest (and most vulnerable) in the realm of recording, mic cables must be of the highest caliber.

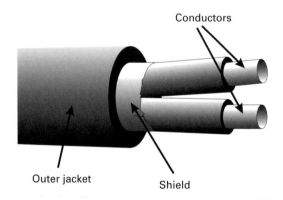

Because the mic signal is one of the smallest
(and most vulnerable) in the realm of recording,
mic cables must be of the highest caliber.

The first line of defense against stray signals is the shield, a sleeve of foil or braided wire that completely encloses the cable's main conductor (see Figure 1.8). This shield does just what its name implies: It intercepts noise and carries it harmlessly away from the conductor. If a mic cable has an inadequate or damaged shield, this protection is compromised. When a conductor has no shield at all, we sometimes give it a different name: an antenna!

Figure 1.8. A cable's shield wraps completely around the signal-carrying conductor(s), protecting them from stray electromagnetic noise.

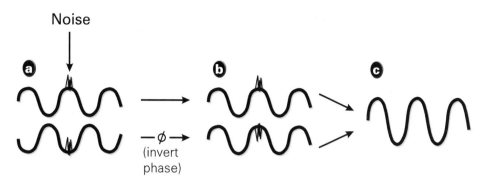

Noise

a   **b**   **c**

—ϕ→
(invert
phase)

Figure 1.9. When noise hits a balanced cable, it affects both the normal and the inverted signal (a). When the mixer or mic preamp puts the inverted signal back to normal (b), the noise cancels itself out (c).

BALANCED SIGNAL

Even wrapped in a metal shield, the mic signal is not impervious to noise. To reduce noise that gets past the shield, we rely on our second line of defense: the balanced cable. Balanced wiring uses three conductors to carry the ground (shield) and both a normal and an out-of-phase version of the original signal. When noise gets through the shield, it affects both signals in the same way. At the recorder or mixer, the mic preamp flips the out-of-phase signal (and any noise it may be carrying) to match the original signal. The two mic signals are now in phase, and any noise present on the two conductors is out of phase. Combining the two signals results in a boosted mic signal, while the noise basically cancels itself out of existence. Because balanced wiring is easier pictured than described, see Figure 1.9.

For long cable runs, balanced wiring is the only way to go.

Though the vast majority of professional mics use balanced wiring, there are some inexpensive mics available with unbalanced connectors. The best way to tell if a mic is balanced or unbalanced is to examine the connector. If the mic has a three-pin XLR connector on its base, it's most likely a balanced mic. If the mic has a permanently attached (or screw-on) cable that ends in a standard tip-sleeve ¼-inch phone jack, the mic is unbalanced.

Professional mics use balanced lines for good reason, and you may want to avoid unbalanced mics due to their higher susceptibility to noise. That said, unbalanced mics may work fine for short cable runs in areas where RF (radio frequency) noise is not a problem. For long cable runs—20 feet or more—balanced wiring is the only way to go.

IMPEDANCE

Another electrical characteristic of microphones that has a marked effect on sound quality is impedance. Impedance measures the internal resistance of a mic to changing voltage (which pretty well describes the mic signal). Most professional mics are low-impedance designs, with impedance specs below about 600 ohms

XLR   1/4-inch   1/4-inch   1/8-inch
        tip-ring-sleeve tip-sleeve   tip-sleeve

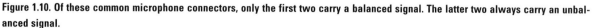

Figure 1.10. Of these common microphone connectors, only the first two carry a balanced signal. The latter two always carry an unbalanced signal.

and typically under 200 ohms. Inexpensive dynamic mics—especially those with permanently attached cables—are usually high impedance, with impedance ratings of 10K (or 10,000) ohms or higher. Some inexpensive mics can have impedance figures as high as 30K ohms.

Without getting too technical, the impedance of a microphone interacts with the *capacitance* found in every mic cable. This interaction causes a reduction of high frequencies, the severity of which increases with mic impedance and cable length. In other words, a high-impedance mic will usually cause a noticeable dulling of the sound if attached to a cable longer than 20 or 30 feet. A low-impedance mic, on the other hand, will exhibit no audible high-frequency loss even if attached to several hundred feet of high-quality cable.

In general, you want to match your mic's impedance to the impedance of the connecting input. Mic inputs on certain (usually inexpensive) equipment work best with high-impedance mics attached; these inputs frequently have unbalanced ¼-inch connectors. XLR inputs are almost always balanced, low-impedance inputs. Plugging a high-impedance mic into a low-impedance input (or vice versa) will almost guarantee a compromised signal.

IMPEDANCE-MATCHING TRANSFORMERS

Though not the best solution, impedance-matching transformers will bump up the effective impedance of a low-impedance mic or lower that of a high-impedance mic. High-to-low impedance transformers balance the normally unbalanced signal of a high-impedance mic, making longer cable runs possible. By using a transformer, you get the advantages of a balanced, low-impedance line with a high-impedance mic.

Low-to-high impedance transformers allow the connection of a professional low-impedance mic to a high-impedance unbalanced input (like that found on many four-track recorders). These transformers also unbalance the signal properly, cancelling noise right at the input. Don't be deceived by a mic cable that has an XLR connector at the mic end and a ¼-inch connector at the other. These cables rarely have a transformer in them; instead, they simply use half of the balanced connection. This negates the noise-cancelling effect of the balanced cable and doesn't properly raise the impedance of the mic.

CHAPTER 2

Microphone Types

How do you tell one mic from the next? It's elemental!

You don't have to spend much time learning about mics to discover that they come in an almost bewildering array of different shapes, styles and sizes. Without some intelligent way to classify mics, we'd have to use statements like, "Give me that long, skinny black mic—it always sounds good on banjo."

Thankfully, it's easy to divide the microphone world into smaller categories based on two main characteristics. The first is how the mic converts air pressure changes (sound) into an electrical signal. This depends on the construction and design of what's at the very heart of the microphone: the *element* (or capsule). Element type divides the mic kingdom into three or four subsets and is the topic of this chapter.

The second way we categorize mics is by specifying how (or whether) the mic favors sounds coming from certain directions. We call this mic characteristic "pickup pattern" or "directional pattern." I'll explore this in more detail in Chapter 4.

The Element

The mic element is the part of the mic that changes one form of energy into another (we call anything that does this a *transducer*). In the case of a microphone, the element responds to changes in air pressure and produces a corresponding change in voltage (see Figure 2.1). This changing voltage makes up the microphone signal, which travels through the microphone cable for amplification, processing and recording.

There are three common element types used in recording: *dynamic, condenser* and *ribbon*. Each element type uses a different method for converting sound into an electrical signal, and each has its own unique characteristics. Of these three, the dynamic and condenser elements are most commonly found in the mic cabinets of home and professional studios.

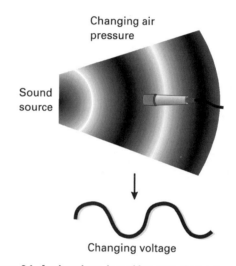

There are three common element types used in recording: dynamic, condenser and ribbon.

Changing air pressure

Sound source

Changing voltage

Figure 2.1. A microphone is nothing more than a transducer that converts changes in air pressure to a changing electrical voltage.

THE DYNAMIC ELEMENT

Condenser and dynamic mics both pick up sound with an extremely thin, light membrane called a *diaphragm,* but this is where the similarities end. Condenser mics rely on an electrical principle called capacitance to generate an electrical signal. (Old-guard engineers often use the terms "condenser" and "capacitor" interchangeably—they both mean the same thing.) Dynamic mics work like a loudspeaker in reverse, relying on *inductance* to create an electrical signal (see Figure 2.2).

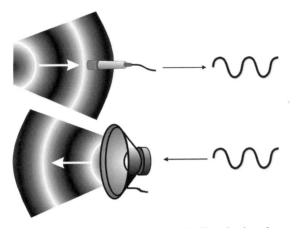

Figure 2.2. The dynamic mic element works like a loudspeaker in reverse, using inductance to create an electrical signal.

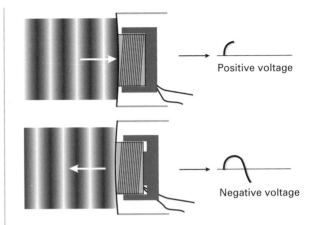

Positive voltage

Negative voltage

Figure 2.4. As the dynamic mic's diaphragm responds to sound, its coil of wire moves through the magnetic field. This creates an electrical current in proportion to diaphragm movement.

In a dynamic mic, the diaphragm attaches to a coil of ultra-fine wire called the voice coil. Surrounding this voice coil is a magnet (see Figure 2.3). As the diaphragm moves in response to sound, the coil of wire moves through the magnetic field. This induces current in proportion to the movement of the diaphragm, creating a signal in the coil of wire (see Figure 2.4). Unlike a condenser mic, the amount of current (or voltage) produced by the dynamic mic is adequate to drive a microphone preamp directly.

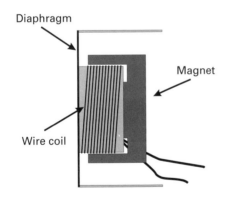

Diaphragm

Magnet

Wire coil

Figure 2.3. Like a loudspeaker, the dynamic element suspends a coil of wire in a magnetic field.

There are two main types of magnets used in today's dynamic mics: iron and neodymium. Traditional iron magnets are cheaper to manufacture, but have less magnetism by weight. Neodymium magnets cost more to make, but create a stronger magnetic field. This makes a more sensitive, higher output microphone, a benefit that has prompted many manufacturers to switch to neodymium magnets in their better dynamic mics.

Dynamic mics, by nature of their design, are among the most rugged mics in use today. They are virtually impervious to temperature and humidity changes and hold up well to physical abuse. (There's a running joke among live sound engineers about being able to drive nails with a certain popular dynamic mic during the day and sing with it at night.)

Dynamic mics, by nature of their design, are among the most rugged mics in use today.

This ruggedness makes dynamics well-suited for the rigors of live sound—the vast majority of singers use handheld dynamic mics on-stage. In the studio, engineers usually reach for a dynamic if there's a chance the mic could get hit by something (like a drumstick). It takes quite an impact to disable a dynamic mic, and a critical blow may only set you back a few hundred dollars. Having a musician crush the life out of an expensive condenser mic is considerably more painful.

Most dynamic mics handle extremely high volumes without distorting. This makes them useful in recording situations where sound pressure levels are intense, such as close-miking guitar amplifiers and drums. The ability of the dynamic mic to put out a healthy signal without a power source makes them one of the only options for recording setups that lack phantom power (more on phantom power later).

Because it's attached to a coil of wire and the paraphernalia that hold this coil in place, the dynamic mic's diaphragm assembly is relatively heavy by microphone standards. Dynamic diaphragms also tend to be much thicker than those of condenser designs, sometimes as much as ten times the thickness. This makes for some definite limitations in mic design and performance. First off, dynamic mics must have a reasonably large diaphragm to generate enough movement for a strong signal. Shrinking the diaphragm greatly reduces the sensitivity of a dynamic mic, which is why so few extremely small microphones use a dynamic element.

The greater mass of the diaphragm assembly can impact a dynamic mic's frequency response. Though not strictly a function of diaphragm mass, dynamic mics generally have an abbreviated high-frequency response as compared to condenser mics. The low-frequency response of dynamic mics tends to be less than that of condenser mics as well. As I'll explore in later chapters, the more limited response of the dynamic mic doesn't necessarily make it any less useful in the studio.

Directly tied to a mic's frequency response is its transient response. In the case of the dynamic mic, the greater mass of the dynamic mic's diaphragm can slow the whole assembly down when reacting to the onset (or transient) of a sound. This has the effect of reducing the attack or crispness of sounds picked up by the microphone. For this reason, most dynamic mics have a less open and transparent sound than condenser mics. Like limited frequency response, though, a little sluggishness in a mic can be an advantage when recording certain sounds.

THE CONDENSER ELEMENT

In order to understand the inner workings of condenser mics, it's best to start with how a capacitor works. In a capacitor, a very thin insulator (or dielectric) sits between two conductive plates. With electricity applied, the two plates are essentially connected in spite of the insulator between them. If you moved one of the plates slightly, the voltage between the two plates would change to reflect the change in distance.

What if we measured the voltage between the two plates as one moved in response to tiny changes in air pressure? If the plate were able to move quickly enough, the resulting voltage would mimic the sound hitting the plate. This is the exact principle behind the condenser mic. The moving plate is the mic's diaphragm, and the stationary plate is the mic's backplate. As the diaphragm moves in response to sound, the voltage between it and the backplate changes (see Figure 2.5). With a little amplification, this changing voltage becomes the mic signal.

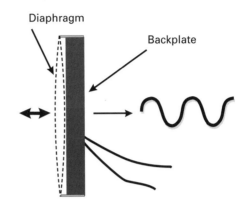

Figure 2.5. As a condenser element's diaphragm moves relative to the backplate, changes in capacitance generate a small electrical signal.

There are several methods for creating condenser diaphragms, depending on the mic's price point. Common in more expensive condensers is a gold-sputtered polyester film diaphragm (see Figure 2.6). Gold-sputtered diaphragms have a microscopic gold layer deposited on them by an electrode. This extremely thin and light conductive layer has excellent electrical characteristics and resistance to corrosion. Some inexpensive condenser mics use a layer of gold, but not one applied in such a meticulous, controlled process. This thicker, less uniform layer generally has poorer acoustic characteristics. Less expensive (and smaller) diaphragms often use a layer of metal alloy over a much thicker membrane.

The resulting signal from the condenser element is extremely weak, even by microphone standards. Because of this, condenser mics have an amplifier built into them (see Figure 2.7). Not to be confused with the preamps found in mixing consoles and outboard units, the condenser mic's built-in amp stage boosts the element's output to a level roughly equivalent to that of a dynamic mic and brings the element's impedance down to a few hundred ohms.

Figure 2.6. The condenser element picks up sound on an ultra-thin diaphragm that is actually one plate of a capacitor. (Courtesy Neumann USA)

Figure 2.7. Because a condenser element puts out such a small voltage, condenser mics have on-board electronics to amplify the signal. (Courtesy Neumann USA)

All amplifiers, including those inside condenser mics, require a power source. Depending on their design, condenser mics have two different ways that they can receive the necessary power. One is a battery placed inside the body of the mic. Usually a normal AA or AAA cell, this battery drives the inner workings of the mic. Condenser preamps don't draw much power; most batteries will work for several hundred hours before replacement. Less expensive condenser mics often require an internal battery, especially those models designed for on-stage use.

It's more common for professional condenser mics to use phantom power. Phantom power is a DC voltage (usually 48 volts) supplied by a mixer or mic preamp. Phantom power goes down the mic cable itself; the preamp then filters out the DC voltage from the microphone's output signal. External supplies are available for mixers that lack phantom power. These supplies are connected between the mic and the console preamp input; most plug into a wall outlet for power (see Figure 2.8). Some external phantom power supplies use batteries for field recording.

Figure 2.8. An external phantom power supply will allow the use of a condenser mic with any mic input. (Courtesy AKG Acoustics)

Many mixers have a single master phantom power switch that precludes you from applying phantom power to individual mics. This means that any dynamic mics plugged into the mixer will receive phantom power as well as the condenser mics. Some manufacturers say that long-term application of phantom power to dynamic mics can cause damage, others say it's no problem. But there is one thing that everyone agrees on: Never plug or unplug a mic with phantom power engaged. This can damage the condenser mic's electronics.

Condenser mics generally have an extended high-frequency response.

In order for the condenser mic's element to function, there must be a DC voltage present on the plate behind the diaphragm (the backplate). There are two methods to achieve this voltage. The most common uses the DC voltage from the phantom power supply. The other method is to use a condenser that contains its own permanent electrical charge (called an electret). Once thought to deliver inferior performance, electret elements are now showing up in many mid-priced microphones. Thanks to advances in manufacturing techniques, audio quality of the modern electret is virtually on a par with that of externally polarized elements.

Because the condenser diaphragm has no coil of wire attached, it can be as much as 20 times lighter than that of a dynamic mic. This affects the condenser mic's performance, making most condensers better able to capture natural, accurate recordings. For one, condenser mics generally have an extended high-frequency response, often extending well beyond the human hearing range.

This high-frequency extension corresponds to a fast transient response, which allows the condenser mic to reliably capture the critical first instant of a sound. The ear often perceives this fast attack as a more crisp and transparent sound, especially on percussive instruments. Also, lighter diaphragms are less likely to ring or resonate at an audible frequency after the sound has passed.

The low mass of the condenser mic diaphragm also contributes to its high sensitivity. The more sensitive the mic, the stronger and more noise-free a signal it produces for a given sound pressure level. Higher sensitivity means a much cleaner signal when recording quiet sounds, making condenser mics the first choice for many softer instruments and voices.

Condenser elements make up both the smallest and the largest diaphragms found in the microphone world; and diaphragm size plays a key role in the sound of the condenser mic (see Figure 2.9). The smallest diaphragms used in studio mics may be as small as 3/16 of an inch. These offer extremely transparent, accurate sound with an unrivaled transient response. Some tiny condenser mics are used as measurement mics due to their extremely flat frequency response.

Figure 2.9. Condenser diaphragms cover a broad range of sizes, from under 3/16 of an inch to well over two inches in diameter.

Large-diaphragm condenser mics may have diaphragms of two inches in diameter or larger, though sizes closer to one inch are most common. These mics usually capture excellent vocal or instrument sounds, and engineers use them more for their unique character than their accuracy. Extremely large-diaphragm condenser mics rarely offer the extended frequency response or fast transient response of smaller diaphragms, but they can create a full, rich, "larger than life" sound.

Condenser mics designed for instrument recording usually fall somewhere in between these size extremes, with diaphragms roughly 3/8 to 1/2 of an inch in diameter. These mics offer a good blend of sensitivity and sound quality. Most condenser instrument mics have a very flat frequency response with extended high- and low-frequency pickup. Though there's no established standard, mics with diaphragms of ½-inch in diameter or smaller are generally considered to be "small-diaphragm" designs. Mic diaphragms of one inch qualify a mic as a "large-diaphragm" design, while everything in between ½ and one inch often bears the label "mid-sized diaphragm."

For all its sonic advantages, the condenser mic does have a few drawbacks. The first is fragility. Though manufacturers have succeeded in making condenser mics sturdier over the years, modern condensers still don't bear rough treatment well. Diaphragms can rip or shift out of alignment if the mic falls, and a strong blast of air can permanently cripple a diaphragm. Most good-quality condenser mics come with a sturdy, padded case; it's a good idea to keep the mic there when not in use. When you're done recording, pull condenser mics from their stands first, before disaster strikes. You don't need to treat condenser mics like delicate porcelain, but they do require more care than most dynamic mics.

*For all its sonic advantages,
the condenser mic does have
a few drawbacks.*

Condenser mics tend to be more susceptible to changes in humidity and temperature than dynamic mics. Extremely moist conditions can dramatically affect the sound of the condenser mic, as can very cold or very hot environments. It's common for recording engineers to be unable to recreate the specific sound of a recording due to changes in humidity or temperature. If a condenser mic doesn't sound like it should, the problem may be in the air.

Drawbacks aside, condenser mics are the workhorses of the modern studio. The reason is simple: Well-designed condenser mics sound great on most any instrument or voice. Because they're so versatile, even the most basic home studio can benefit from having at least one good-quality condenser mic.

THE RIBBON ELEMENT

Ribbon mics use a different method to pick up sound, one which offers some of the advantages of both condenser and dynamic mics. Much like a dynamic mic, ribbon mics rely on a magnet, a moving conductor and the electrical property of inductance to create a signal. Like a condenser mic, most ribbon mics have a smooth, broad frequency response due to a relatively low-mass transducer.

Instead of a round diaphragm, a ribbon mic suspends a narrow strip of metal (a foil ribbon) inside a magnet assembly (see Figure 2.10). This ribbon vibrates in response to sound, creating a signal as it moves through the magnetic field. The resulting signal is strong enough to drive a mixer's microphone input, so the ribbon mic needs no on-board preamp. Like the dynamic mic, the ribbon mic works without phantom power or a built-in battery. The application of phantom power will actually destroy certain ribbon microphones.

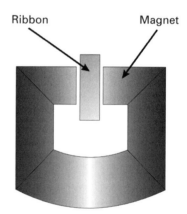

Figure 2.10. A ribbon element suspends an ultra-thin ribbon in a powerful magnetic field. As the ribbon moves in response to air, it creates an electrical current in proportion to the diaphragm's movement.

Ribbon mics use different sized ribbons, though most are roughly ⅛ of an inch wide and about an inch long. Because the actual ribbon is so thin, ribbon mics are quite fragile. A strong puff of air can tear the ribbon from its mount. Even carrying the mic unprotected can subject it to damaging airflow. Breath pops from vocalists have destroyed many ribbon mics, making the external pop filter a necessity. Ribbon mics rarely show up in live sound situations, though vocalists will sometimes use a handheld ribbon mic on stage. Studio use of ribbons is more common, but they still need special care.

There is a common misconception that ribbon mics don't handle loud sounds well. In actuality, the ability of a ribbon mic to handle high sound pressure levels depends on the frequency of the sound. Low-frequency sounds require broader swings of the ribbon to achieve the same electrical output, which quickly limits the ribbon's max SPL. At higher frequencies (above 100Hz, for example), a ribbon can withstand sound pressure levels in excess of 130dB. At midrange and treble frequencies, a ribbon's max SPL can jump to 150 or 160dB.

Ribbon mics generally have an open, accurate sound, much like that of condenser mics.

When a dynamic or condenser mic overloads, there's rarely damage done to the element; when a ribbon mic overloads, permanent damage is a definite possibility. When the ribbon deflects far enough to rub against nearby metal or screen, it can alter the ribbon's sound in subtle (or not-so-subtle) ways. In the worst case, a loud sound can break the ribbon free of its mount or stretch the ribbon enough to dramatically change its sound.

Ribbon mics have an open, accurate sound, much like that of condenser mics. The lightweight ribbon responds readily to sound, giving most ribbon mics good high-frequency and transient response characteristics. The frequency responses of ribbon mics tend to be very even, with few unwanted resonances in the audible band. Older ribbon mics with thicker diaphragms may exhibit less transient detail and high-frequency extension—these vintage models are known for their very smooth sound quality.

CHAPTER 3

Specialty Mics

Some out-of-the-ordinary mics that can give you extraordinary sounds.

The vast majority of mics used in today's home studios are either dynamic, condenser or ribbon designs—and for good reason. Dynamic and condenser mics have proven themselves to be recording workhorses, offering excellent sound and reliability at a reasonable cost. It's not often that the home recordist comes across a recording situation that one of these mics can't handle. And ribbon mics, though not nearly as popular, see regular use in a fair number of home studios.

Beyond these, there are several other types of microphones—some of them variations on common designs—that you should know about. While often not as versatile (or affordable) as the three mic types listed above, these specialty mics have applications where they may capture a better recording than a standard mic.

BOUNDARY MICS

The first (and perhaps most common) specialty mic of interest to the home studio owner is the "pressure zone" or boundary microphone. The boundary mic is essentially a condenser diaphragm mounted in a novel way to eliminate the comb filter effects of combined direct and reflected sound. A small condenser diaphragm (usually an electret) is suspended just above a flat plate (see Figure 3.1). Because the diaphragm is right against a reflecting surface, all sounds are arriving direct and are free from delayed reflections. And because it's picking up sound both arriving at and reflecting away from the boundary plate, the boundary mic benefits from a phenomenon called "pressure doubling." This raises the boundary mic's sensitivity by 6dB.

Boundary mics, by design, usually have a hemispherical pickup pattern.

The boundary mic is the only type of microphone that has an implied pickup pattern. Dynamic, condenser or ribbon mics can have any number of different pickup patterns. Boundary mics, by design, usually have a hemispherical pickup pattern. This is the result of an otherwise normal omnidirectional sphere pattern cut down the middle by the mic's boundary plate.

Figure 3.1. Electro-Voice CT-30 boundary mic. (Courtesy EV)

Some boundary mics offer a modified half-cardioid pattern, which is also split down the middle. This greater directivity allows manufacturers to place several elements on one boundary plate, creating a sort of multi-pattern mic. Often used on conference tables, these mics allow users to turn on or disable individual elements to tailor the pickup response.

The high-frequency response of the boundary mic usually matches that of any good-quality condenser mic. Low-frequency response, on the other hand, depends on one significant variable: the size of the boundary plate. The smaller the boundary plate, the poorer the mic's low-frequency response. The average attached boundary plate (around five square inches) allows the boundary mic to have a low-frequency response flat to several hundred Hertz. To pick up strong bass down to around 100Hz, the boundary plate needs to be several feet across.

Fortunately, one doesn't have to purchase a special boundary from the manufacturer to get good low-frequency response. Any flat surface the mic sits on will extend the boundary plate, be it studio ceil-

16

ing, 4x4-foot piece of plywood or glass window. Boundary microphones also work well when placed on the floor near an instrument.

Well-designed boundary mics generally have a clear, uncolored response. Placed on a wall, floor or ceiling, a boundary mic can record an uncannily real representation of sound in a room. Without an additional boundary to extend the low-frequency response, the boundary mic is useful for recording cymbals or other high-frequency sounds. Some engineers have had good results placing a boundary mic inside a bass drum. In fact, at least one company makes a boundary mic designed specifically for kick drum applications. It's not uncommon in home studios to find boundary mics permanently attached to the ceiling for drum kit recording or mounted inside the lid or on the sounding board of a grand piano.

Because the boundary mic uses a type of condenser diaphragm, it needs a source of power to operate. Some mics contain a 1.5-volt battery, while others use phantom power from a mixer, recorder or preamp. Most boundary mics designed for professional use accept a balanced XLR connector.

LAVALIER MICS

Another type of condenser design is the lavalier or lav mic. Designed to be inconspicuous when pinned to a shirt or concealed under clothing, lav mics have an extremely small condenser diaphragm (see Figure 3.2). This gives them a very fast transient response but relatively low sensitivity. Most lavalier mics have an omnidirectional pickup pattern, though cardioid (or tighter) designs are becoming more common.

Figure 3.2. Though usually designed for picking up speech, lavalier mics work well in certain recording applications. (Courtesy Crown International)

Most lavalier mics are electret designs, requiring power only for their on-board preamplifiers. A 1.5-volt battery is the most common lavalier power supply, usually sitting in a small box or tube that connects to the mic with a fine wire. As with other electret designs, you can expect a lavalier's battery to last for hundreds (or even thousands) of hours.

The crisp, open sound of most lavaliers make them useful for picking up more than just speech. Engineers have had success using these little mics for many instrument recording applications, often placing them where larger mics wouldn't fit. The small, clip-on instrument mics that are growing more popular have much in common with the lavalier. It's not a bad idea to have a small lavalier mic or two available for the occasional out-of-the-ordinary miking application.

The crisp, open sound of most lavaliers make them useful for picking up more than just speech.

TUBE MICS

There's no denying that vacuum tube electronics have staged a massive comeback in the recording studio. With the advent of solid-state electronics, transistors and operational amplifiers (op-amps) in recent decades, tube audio circuits seemed doomed to extinction. Instead of disappearing, however, many of today's engineers prize vintage and modern tube gear for its warm, rich sound. Tubes, their proponents say, have much more musical characteristics than their silicon counterparts. Manufacturers have been happy to oblige this tube renaissance, offering tube circuits in every kind of product from microphone to spring reverb (see Figure 3.3).

Since the audio tube is primarily a device that supplies amplification (gain) to an electrical signal, the only mic type that commonly sports an internal tube is the condenser. In tube condenser mics, the tube lowers the extremely high impedance of the condenser capsule to a more usable level, usually boosting the small output from the diaphragm in the process. Transistors or op-amps generally handle these chores in non-tube condenser mics. The end result is the same: The mic generates a signal of adequate strength to survive the trip down the microphone cable.

Figure 3.3. The AKG C-12VR tube microphone. (Courtesy AKG Acoustics)

The main area where tube mics differ from conventional condensers is their power requirements. Tubes generally require a relatively high DC voltage to operate, considerably higher than the 48 volts available through traditional phantom power supplies. Hence, most tube condenser mics use an external power supply that plugs directly into an AC outlet (see Figure 3.4). A special cable carries the high DC voltage to the mic and returns the mic signal to the supply; a standard mic cable plugs into the supply to carry the mic signal to the mixer or recorder. On multi-pattern tube mics, you'll often find the pattern selection switch on the remote power supply instead of the mic itself.

Figure 3.4. Tube mic power supply—note remote pickup pattern selector at left. (Courtesy Event Electronics)

In use, the tube mic has few special considerations. The gain and noise performance of some tube mics stabilizes after a short warm-up interval before recording. It's a good idea to power up these mics for at least 5 minutes, and 15 or 20 minutes is preferred. After that, a tube mic's case may be warmer to the touch than a standard condenser. The tube usually warms up the whole microphone, which can help drive away troublesome moisture.

Ironically, some tubes used in microphones can be *microphonic* themselves, meaning they generate an audible sound in response to physical movement. A mic with a microphonic tube will be more sensitive to knocks or bumps and should be treated with extra care to avoid unwanted noises. Tubes may become more microphonic as they age.

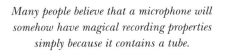

Many people believe that a microphone will somehow have magical recording properties simply because it contains a tube.

Tubes used in such low-power applications as microphones often have a life span measured in decades, though some may fail after just a few years of use. Most tubes fail as a result of mechanical shock; those that don't usually blow when first powered on. For this reason, it's best to be gentle with a powered-up tube mic. Avoiding unnecessary on/off cycles can also extend tube life. If a tube begins to deteriorate due to age, the mic may become noisy or distort at low sound pressure levels.

There are many misconceptions about tube mics. The first is that all tube mics have a warmer sound, usually implying a somewhat rolled-off high-frequency response. A tube mic may have a slightly attenuated high-frequency response, but rarely as a result of the tube itself. Well-designed tube-based circuits can easily match the high-end frequency response of solid-state audio components, and some tube mics have a very detailed, bright sound.

The second misconception involves noise. Some feel that tube mics are noisier than solid-state models. Though certain tube mics do exhibit higher degrees of self-noise, this is not a characteristic of all tube mics.

Lastly, many people believe that a microphone will somehow have magical recording properties simply because it contains a tube. In reality, a tube pre-amp circuit has a much less pronounced effect on a mic's sound than the design of the diaphragm and related components. Most great tube mics would be great mics regardless of whether they had a tube in them. Likewise, adding a tube to a poorly designed mic will not make up for the mic's inadequacies.

Tube mics are generally expensive, for reasons largely unrelated to the cost of the vacuum tube itself. The high-voltage power supply required by the mic bumps up manufacturing costs, as does the larger physical size of most tube mics. The real cost issue, however, lies in the tendency of manufacturers to put tubes only in mics at or near the top of their product line. This adds to the perceived value of these already premium models. There are some exceptions to the high-cost trend in tube mics, several of which are listed in Section 6.

Many lower-budget recordists question whether tube mics are worth their higher price tag. If you like the character of a given tube mic and can justify the purchase price, it's a good investment. If a tube doesn't sound the best for your application, purchasing the mic on the basis of its tube electronics isn't the best decision. When it comes to choosing and using a microphone, its sound—not its type of electronics—should be your number one criterion.

HIGH-VOLTAGE MICS

In your recording travels, you may come across condenser mics referred to as "high-voltage" models. These mics are usually small-diaphragm designs with ultra-flat frequency responses. Their higher cost and somewhat esoteric nature puts them out of reach for most home studios.

Instead of using a standard phantom power supply (around 48 volts DC), these mics require a special supply capable of upwards of 130 volts DC. This higher DC voltage feeds specially designed electronics in the mic that have lower noise than standard designs. The end result is a cleaner signal from a more sensitive microphone.

Like tube mics, high-voltage condensers pose no special challenge other than their reliance on a special power supply. Some mic preamps available today offer a high-voltage supply to drive such mics, though these preamps tend to be on the higher end of the price scale. Other operating characteristics of high-voltage mics are identical to those of the standard condenser.

Like tube mics, high-voltage condensers pose no special challenge other than their reliance on a special power supply.

The ruler-flat frequency response of most high-voltage mics makes them well-suited to distant miking of acoustic instruments. Classical recording engineers sometimes use these mics for recording symphonies, choirs and other large ensembles. High-voltage mics are the first choice of some engineers when they need high sensitivity and very low noise.

CONTACT MICS

Unlike regular mics, which respond to changes in air pressure, contact mics or contact transducers respond to the physical vibrations of a solid object. They have to be in physical contact with the instrument being recorded. Some contact mics are small enough to attach to the bridge of an acoustic guitar, while others are long, thin strips that stick to a flat or curved surface on larger instruments (see Figure 3.5).

Figure 3.5. A contact mic sits directly on the instrument, picking up mechanical vibrations instead of sound. (Courtesy AKG Acoustics)

The interface between resonating surfaces and air is a crucial part of any instrument's sonic character. Because a contact mic bypasses the airborne vibration step completely, the signal it generates is rarely a close match to the acoustic sound of the instrument. Contact mics don't necessarily generate a bad sound, just one quite different from what you might expect. Contact mics usually require a fair degree of equalization or other processing to match the acoustic character of the instrument.

Proper placement is the most critical factor in getting a usable signal from a contact mic. Every resonant surface of an instrument carries a different mix of fundamental and overtones; moving a contact mic just a few millimeters can cause a dramatic shift in frequency balance. Locating the "sweet spot" on a instrument—the place that carries the most natural-sounding blend of frequencies—usually requires some trial and error with a contact mic.

Because they don't respond to audible sound, contact mics are useful when you need a high degree of sound rejection, such as miking a piano sitting very close to a drum kit or an acoustic bass in danger of being drowned out by a guitar amp. In some cases, it may be impossible to position a mic for optimum sound due to space restraints. In this case, a contact mic may generate an adequate signal for recording.

Proper placement is the most critical factor in getting a usable signal from a contact mic.

Contact mics are used more for live sound reinforcement than recording. Still, you may come across certain studio applications where the contact mic does a good job either as a main mic or as a supplement to a traditional mic. As a special effect mic to capture a purposely altered recording of an instrument, the contact mic can be very effective.

Most contact mics have a permanently attached cable, often ending in an unbalanced ¼-inch connector. Some contact mics have a standard XLR connector, generating a balanced mic-level signal.

TWO-WAY MICS

As we'll explore in Chapter 5, the relatively small diaphragm of a microphone is much better at controlling high-frequency directivity than lower frequencies. Due to the large difference in wavelength between bass and treble frequencies, it's virtually impossible to design one diaphragm with an even directional response at both ends of the frequency range.

One solution, which has been implemented by a handful of manufacturers, is to put two separate diaphragms in one microphone. One diaphragm is larger than the other (usually about twice the diameter), and a crossover network combines the output of the two. The two-way mic is much like a two-way speaker system where large and small drivers special-

ize in bass and treble frequencies respectively.

Devoting one diaphragm to high frequencies and one to low frequencies makes for a more consistent directional pattern across the audible range. It also creates a more even, extended frequency response at both treble and bass frequencies. The main drawback of the two-way mic is the crossover required to combine the two diaphragms, an additional stage of processing that can generate phase problems and distortion.

The two-way mic works much like a two-way speaker system.

Performance characteristics and specs of the two-way condenser mic will be similar to a normal condenser. In application, you use a two-way mic as you would a standard design. The potential difference lies in sound: A two-way mic can capture the transparent, open treble of a small-diaphragm mic as well as the full, rich sound of a large-diaphragm design.

Because of the additional diaphragm and added complexity of electronics, two-way mics cost appreciably more than their single-diaphragm brethren. The somewhat debatable improvement in sound quality of the two-way mic has kept it from really catching on with manufacturers or recording engineers, while its price has kept it out of most home studios.

CHAPTER 4

Microphone Pickup Patterns

Sometimes a little discrimination is a good thing.

After element type, the most common way to categorize microphones is by pickup pattern (or directional pattern). *Directional* mics are more sensitive to sound coming from certain directions, while *omnidirectional* mics pick up sound equally from all directions. As I'll explore in later chapters, a mic's directional pattern has a dramatic effect on its sound and suitability for certain applications. Before I begin discussing mic pickup patterns, a little theory is in order.

A mic's directional pattern has everything to do with how its element interfaces with the air. In a *pressure-gradient* or *velocity* system, the mic's diaphragm or ribbon has both its front and back surfaces exposed to the air. The diaphragm will only respond to air pressure differences between the front and back surfaces, or the pressure gradient between the two sides. If a sound comes directly from the side of the element, it creates identical air pressure fluctuations on both sides of the diaphragm. Like two people pushing on a swinging door from opposite sides, the result is no movement of the diaphragm—no sound. A true pressure-gradient mic design has a perfect bidirectional pattern.

In a *pressure* system, only one surface of the ribbon or diaphragm is exposed to the air. Any air pressure change, regardless of its direction of travel, will set the diaphragm into motion. We call such a mic "omnidirectional." Every other microphone pattern besides omnidirectional and bidirectional uses a combination of pressure and pressure-gradient operation.

Omnidirectional Mics

Omnidirectional mics (or "omnis" for short) don't discriminate against sounds coming from any direction. Instead, sounds approaching the mic from all directions get identical treatment. The mic's pickup pattern is roughly sphere-shaped (see Figure 4.1). The only place an omni may fail to pick up evenly is where a solid portion of the mic's windscreen (or the mic itself) gets in the way of high-frequency sounds.

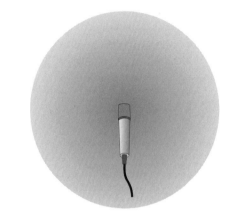

Figure 4.1. An omnidirectional pickup pattern allows the mic to pick up sound equally from all directions.

Omnidirectional mics are the simplest of all the directional patterns, using no electronic or mechanical trickery to alter their sensitivity. Along with the bidirectional ribbon mic, this gives the omni the potential to capture natural, uncolored sound. Omnidirectional mics tend to be free from proximity effect as well, which gives them a very true sound when used close to an instrument or voice. You'll learn more about proximity effect in the next section.

When used indoors, omni mics tend to pick up the most room sound of any directional pattern. This happens because reflected sounds are free to bounce into the mic from all directions, instead of just directly in front of it. Even when placed quite close to the sound source, omnis pick up a healthy amount of room ambience. For this reason, recordists rarely use omni mics when trying to minimize the coloration of a less-than-ideal acoustic space. When good-sounding reverb from the room plays a significant role in the character of the sound, omnidirectional mics work very well.

When used indoors, omni mics tend to pick up the most "room" sound of any directional pattern.

Though it may seem backward at first, omnidirectional mics do not have sound-entry slots behind their diaphragms (see Figure 4.2). Such slots are usually found on directional mics, where sound entering behind the diaphragm is delayed to create cancellation. Instead, omni mics frequently have just a single small opening or grill at the very front. This is consistent with a pressure mic design, which puts just one surface of the mic's diaphragm in contact with the air. This allows the mic to respond to air pressure changes regardless of the direction they're coming from.

Figure 4.2. Though it may seem backward at first, most omni mics have no rear-entry slots (left). Directional mics do. (Courtesy Audio-Technica)

Directional Mics

Though an omnidirectional mic may offer the truest sound pickup, its indiscriminate pickup pattern creates problems in many recording situations. It's common for recordists to pick up one specific instrument while blocking out other sounds, something an omni doesn't do well. With few home studios offering optimum acoustics, *minimizing* the contribution of the room to a recording often becomes a primary goal when selecting a mic.

For these reasons, directional mics are the most frequently used in home and professional studios. Directional mics give the recordists a little more control, allowing him or her to aim the mic to pick up specific sounds and reject others. Within the realm of directional mics, there are several different patterns to choose from. This variety gives the recordist even more control over the recorded sound.

The heart-shaped cardioid pattern is probably the most common directional pattern in use today (see Figure 4.3). The cardioid pattern's main claim to fame is that it offers extremely good rejection of sounds coming from directly behind the mic and some rejection of sounds coming from the sides. Though cardioid patterns differ slightly from model to model, the textbook cardioid pattern reduces rearward sounds by as much as 25dB. Sounds coming from in front of the mic are picked up evenly across a relatively large area (roughly 130 degrees), with no appreciable phase or frequency response unevenness in this broad "sweet spot."

Figure 4.3. The cardioid pattern is most sensitive to sounds coming from directly in front of the mic and least sensitive to those coming from directly behind.

The cardioid pattern offers extremely good rejection of sounds coming from directly behind the mic and some rejection of sounds coming from the sides.

Cardioid pickup patterns are common in both condenser and dynamic mics. When manufacturers lower the price of large-diaphragm condensers by offering just one pickup pattern, it's almost always the cardioid pattern they retain. Likewise, inexpensive dynamic mics almost always offer a basic cardioid pattern; more expensive dynamics are usually available with tighter directional patterns.

SUPERCARDIOID AND HYPERCARDIOID PATTERNS

Supercardioid and hypercardioid pickup patterns are more directional variations on the standard cardioid. The supercardioid pattern tightens up the sensitivity at the front of the mic to about 115 degrees with a tradeoff in rearward rejection (which drops to just 12dB). In other words, as the front pattern gets tighter, sensitivity to sounds directly behind the mic also increases. As compared to the cardioid pattern, the supercardioid mic's area of high rejection splits in two and moves to the sides of the mic (see Figure 4.4).

Figure 4.4. The supercardioid pattern offers more directional pickup in front but adds an area of increased pickup directly behind the mic.

The hypercardioid mic takes this evolution a step further, tightening up the front-facing pattern to just over 100 degrees. The rearward rejection of the mic drops to just 6dB as a result, and the areas of reduced sensitivity move even further toward the sides. The hypercardioid pattern begins to look much like the next pattern I'll discuss: the bidirectional or figure-8 pattern (see Figure 4.5).

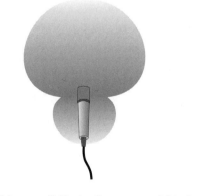

Figure 4.5. A hypercardioid mic offers an even tighter front pattern; the tradeoff is more pickup of sound coming from directly behind the mic.

It's important to understand that supercardioid and hypercardioid mics, though more directional than the cardioid, offer poorer rejection of sounds coming from directly behind them. If the sounds you're trying to suppress are coming from behind the mic, you'll get better rejection from the "looser" cardioid pattern. If the unwanted sounds are coming from behind and to the side, a supercardioid or hypercardioid pattern may give better rejection.

Even more than the cardioid pattern, supercardioid and hypercardioid mics tend to de-emphasize the sound of the room when recording indoors. As a result, you can place a cardioid mic, or one of its variations, twice as far from the sound source as an omni mic and still maintain the same ratio of direct sound to room sound. This ability to reduce room ambience makes sounds recorded with directional mics seem closer to the listener than those recorded with an omni mic at the same distance. You can use this apparent closeness to your advantage, especially when you're trying to get a delicate, intimate sound or a brash, in-your-face effect.

Even more than the cardioid pattern, supercardioid and hypercardioid mics tend to de-emphasize the sound of the room when recording indoors.

BIDIRECTIONAL PATTERN

The bidirectional pattern is exactly what its name implies: a pattern that has two opposing areas of high sensitivity. Shaped like a figure-8, this pickup pattern has a ring of high sound rejection all the way around its perimeter (see Figure 4.6). In that sense, the figure-8 represents the final step in tightening up the front lobe of a cardioid mic and increasing the sensitivity of the back lobe. In the same way that a cardioid mic is less sensitive to sounds entering from behind, the bidirectional mic will almost completely reject sound sources that lie perpendicular to it.

Figure 4.6. A bidirectional mic picks up sound equally from front and back, while offering a high degree of sound rejection at the sides.

A bidirectional microphone is by nature a pressure-gradient system, which exposes both sides of the sensing surface to the air. In reality, only the ribbon microphone can deliver true pressure-gradient operation from a single surface. Sound can never have completely unhindered access to the back of a dynamic diaphragm due to the dynamic mic's coil and magnet assembly. For this reason, bidirectional dynamic mics are almost unheard of.

With condenser mics, the best way to create a true bidirectional pattern is by mounting two diaphragms back-to-back (usually on the same backplate). The mic electrically combines the output of these two capsules, and their proximity makes them function as if they were a single diaphragm. Many condenser mics with a bidirectional pattern are multi-pattern units as well, offering a range of settings between omnidirectional and figure-8. I'll cover multi-pattern mics in more detail in the next section.

SHOTGUN PATTERN

As we've seen in the progression from cardioid pattern to figure-8, the tradeoff in tightening up the forward-facing sensitivity is an increase in the rearward sensitivity. In contrast, shotgun mics have a tight front pattern with very little sound pickup from the back or sides (see Figure 4.7). Most shotgun mics are of a condenser design, relying on phantom power or a built-in battery.

Figure 4.7. A shotgun mic offers a very tight pattern in front, while still offering good rejection of sounds coming from behind.

The shotgun mic gets its name because its long, perforated tube looks like the barrel of a shotgun (see Figure 4.8). This interference tube is the key to the shotgun mic's tight pattern. Sound entering the tube's slots (most of which lie behind the diaphragm) has further to travel to hit the diaphragm than sound entering the front. This delay causes phase cancellation, significantly reducing the level of these sounds.

Figure 4.8. The shotgun mic uses a long interference tube to achieve a high degree of directivity. (Courtesy Audio-Technica)

The long interference tube cancels even low frequencies, allowing the shotgun mic to maintain a tight pattern over a relatively broad frequency range. In general, the longer the shotgun mic's interference tube, the tighter its pickup pattern and the better it rejects low frequencies off-axis. Most shotgun mics with short interference tubes (under about 12 inches) have pickup patterns that look much like that of a standard hypercardioid mic.

Though shotgun mics are some of the most directional mics available, they are rarely used in studio applications. It's not common to need this high a degree of isolation in recording, and the shotgun mic's tight pickup pattern tends to exaggerate any movement of the sound source. Finally, what little sound trickles in to the rear and sides of a shotgun mic is often picked up with significant coloration. This is due to the uneven off-axis frequency and phase responses of most shotgun mics.

Though shotgun mics are some of the most directional mics available, they are rarely used in studio applications.

HEMISPHERE PATTERN

The last pickup pattern I'll cover is the hemisphere or half-sphere pattern (see Figure 4.9). The pressure zone or boundary mic type usually generates a hemispherical pattern as a result of the diaphragm's interaction with the backing plate. The diaphragm picks up sounds coming from above the plate with equal intensity, regardless of direction.

Figure 4.9. A hemisphere pattern offers equal pickup of sounds coming from any direction above the boundary.

Second only to the omnidirectional mic, the hemispherical mic offers one of the least directional pickup patterns. This makes it useful for picking up the ambience or room sound of a given space. If isolation between sounds is your goal, however, the hemisphere pattern is a poor choice.

Figure 4.10 compares key performance characteristics of the most common pickup patterns. Figure 4.11 shows 3-D renderings of three common patterns; these are helpful for understanding how a mic really works.

CHARACTERISTIC	OMNI-DIRECTIONAL	CARDIOID	SUPER-CARDIOID	HYPER-CARDIOID	BI-DIRECTIONAL
POLAR RESPONSE PATTERN	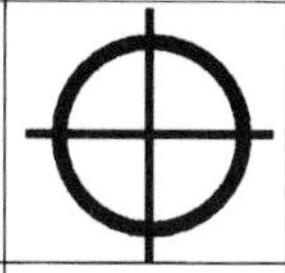		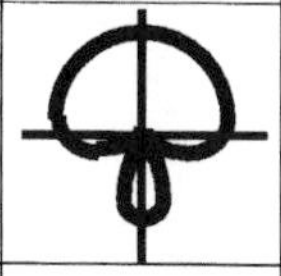		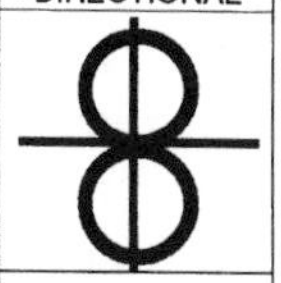
COVERAGE ANGLE	360°	131°	115°	105°	90°
ANGLE OF MAXIMUM REJECTION (null angle)	—	180°	126°	110°	90°
REAR REJECTION (relative to front)	0	25 dB	12 dB	6 dB	0
AMBIENT SOUND SENSITIVITY (relative to omni)	100%	33%	27%	25%	33%
DISTANCE FACTOR (relative to omni)	1	1.7	1.9	2	1.7

Figure 4.10. Key characteristics of the most common mic pickup patterns. (Courtesy Shure Bros.)

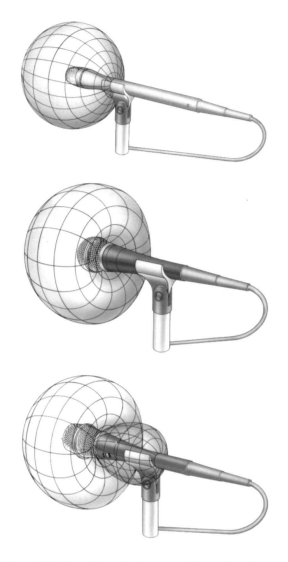

Figure 4.11. Three-dimensional representations of omni, cardioid and supercardioid patterns (from top to bottom). (Courtesy Shure Bros.)

MULTI-PATTERN MICS

The most flexible of all mic designs are those that offer more than one pickup pattern from the same microphone. These mics allow you to tailor the response to the miking situation, making it practical for many home studios to own just one high-quality microphone. For studio recording applications, today's true multi-pattern mics use condenser diaphragms.

The most common way to achieve multiple patterns is by putting two identical diaphragms in one mic. These diaphragms sit back to back, with their outputs wired into a circuit that combines their signals in various ways. The two capsules can then generate omnidirectional, cardioid and figure-8 patterns. Some mics allow intermediate patterns between bi-

directional and cardioid or between omnidirectional and cardioid (see Figure 4.12). Again, these intermediate patterns are simple to create by changing the gain and polarity of the signals from the two diaphragms (see Figure 4.13).

Figure 4.12. Many multi-pattern mics offer between five and ten directional settings, spanning all possible patterns from omni to cardioid to bidirectional. (Courtesy Neumann USA)

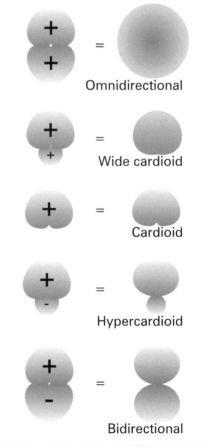

Figure 4.13. By adjusting the level and polarity of two back-to-back diaphragms, multi-pattern mics can create the full range of pickup patterns.

Some mics create multiple patterns with a single diaphragm. Instead of using electronics, these mics use mechanical shutters to plug and unplug holes and chambers behind the diaphragm. These mics usually require a screwdriver to change polar patterns right on the element itself, granting access to the shutter assembly through a hole on the grill of the mic.

On mics with just a few fixed settings, the most common patterns are cardioid, omnidirectional and bidirectional. With these mics, the pattern selector switch is usually on the body of the mic itself. When a mic offers numerous settings between omnidirectional and bidirectional, you'll often find its pattern control on an external box. This box plugs into an AC outlet and provides power to the mic through a special cable. This ends the need for phantom power at the mixer or recorder, allowing you to use multi-pattern mics with a wider range of equipment.

The main advantage of the multi-pattern mic is its flexibility. You can easily change from one pattern to another for miking different instruments or experiment with different settings on the same source. If a vocal sounds too dark due to proximity effect in the cardioid pattern, a multi-pattern mic allows you to quickly select an intermediate pattern between cardioid and omnidirectional.

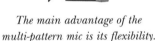

The main advantage of the multi-pattern mic is its flexibility.

A less-convenient multi-pattern system is found on mics with interchangeable capsules. With these mics, you can usually purchase omnidirectional, cardioid or hypercardioid capsules that attach to the front of the mic body (see Figure 4.14). The main advantage is lower cost: The price of these mics with one capsule is usually lower than that of a true multi-pattern mic, and the additional capsules cost much less than an additional mic. Mics with interchangeable capsules are almost always small-diaphragm condenser designs.

Though interchangeable capsules are an inexpensive way to acquire a versatile mic, there are disadvantages. The first is changeover time: Unscrewing a capsule and attaching another is much more time-consuming than simply moving a switch or turning a knob. Second, interchangeable capsules can be somewhat fragile. Improper handling can damage the capsule, and it's relatively easy to mis-thread the capsule and harm the threads on some mics.

Figure 4.14. An interchangeable capsule system gives you numerous pickup pattern choices without the need to buy several mics. (Courtesy Audix)

Most large-diaphragm mics have their capsule(s) mounted in line with the body of the mic. This side-address or side-firing design allows sound to hit both sides of the capsule assembly, a necessity for bidirectional pickup patterns. Small-diaphragm condenser mics usually have their diaphragms mounted perpendicular to the mic body in an axial arrangement (sometimes called "end-fire"), blocking access to the back of the diaphragm (see Figure 4.15). For this reason, most interchangeable capsule designs do not offer a bidirectional pickup pattern.

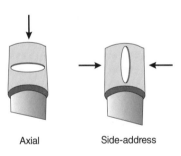

Axial   Side-address

Figure 4.15. Axial or end-fire mics pick up sound on-axis with the mic body (left). Side-address or side-fire mics are most sensitive to sound coming from perpendicular to the mic body (right).

CHAPTER 5

Microphone Performance

All mics are not created equal.

Here's what separates the great performers from the paperweights.

When choosing which microphone to use on a particular instrument or voice, we're rarely concerned with the mic's size or how its finish is holding up. Mic selection is all about using a mic that brings out the best sound in your recording. If a highly esteemed, big-buck mic nets you a poor-sounding recording, it's the wrong mic for the job.

It's helpful to be able to quantify microphone performance. We do this in various ways, some coldly scientific and some highly subjective. It's simple enough to measure a microphone's frequency response with the right equipment. It's not so easy to quantify whether a given mic imparts enough "air" to an acoustic guitar. In this chapter, I'll examine the scientific ways of measuring a microphone's performance, with an eye towards how these specs affect real-world recordings. The subjective aspects of microphone performance are up to you to decide; I'll talk more about these in later chapters.

Before I begin, it's worth noting that specs don't even come close to telling you the whole story about a microphone. Some of the most popular mics don't have stellar specifications, and many mics with perfect specs never leave their foam-lined coffins. Until you hear a mic in action, there's no real way to predict its performance. Still, specifications are a valid way to learn about certain aspects of mic performance.

FREQUENCY RESPONSE

Frequency response is one of the most common microphone specifications. This tells you the highest and lowest frequencies that the mic can pick up and usually states how far the mic's response has dropped at those extremes. If a manufacturer gives you only one spec on a mic, it will probably be frequency response.

The more effectively a mic covers the full human hearing range, the better it will capture sounds without coloration. If a mic doesn't reach beyond 12 or 13kHz on the top end, it may be reducing critical high frequencies. This can result in a dulling of the sound and a loss of high-frequency openness and clarity. Likewise, a mic whose response bottoms out at just 80Hz won't capture the deepest bass notes from certain instruments.

The more effectively a mic covers the full human hearing range, the better it will capture sounds without coloration.

A printed specification, such as "60Hz to 17kHz, +/-3dB" says the mic's frequency response can vary as much as 3dB more or 3dB less than an absolute flat response at which the mic would reproduce all frequencies between 60 and 17,000Hz at a consistent level. However, in most cases, the frequency response spec indicates that the mic's bass response has fallen 3dB at 60Hz, and its high-frequency response is down 3dB at 17kHz. Mics continue to pick up some sound above and below the stated cutoff point, though the mic's sensitivity decreases rapidly past these extremes. Three decibels is the standard roll-off that most manufacturers measure, though some use a 6dB-down point to make their specs look better. If one mic is down 6dB at 16kHz and a second mic is down 3dB at 16kHz, for example, the latter mic will have considerably better high-frequency response.

Other than stating the upper and lower limits of a mic's pickup, the text frequency response spec doesn't tell you much. There's no way to tell how smooth the mic's response is between these two extremes or how quickly its response declines past the cutoff points. Factor in the tendency for manufacturers to fudge frequency response specs in their favor, and the result is a nearly meaningless set of numbers (see Figure 5.1).

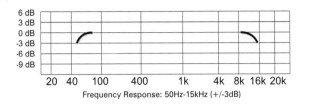

Frequency Response: 50Hz-15kHz (+/-3dB)

Figure 5.1. A printed frequency response specification actually tells you very little about the mic's performance.

Much more informative than the text specification is a frequency response chart. This chart shows you the mic's response across the human hearing range, allowing the experienced eye to spot certain characteristics of the mic's sound. A rising response in the upper-mid and treble range, for example, often means a mic will sound bright and detailed. A subtly rolled-off high-frequency response is common in mics with a smooth or warm character. More dramatic peaks or dips in a mic's response will give clues to that mic's unique sonic signature (see Figure 5.2).

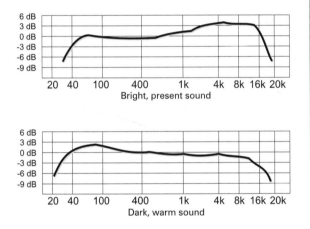

Bright, present sound

Dark, warm sound

Figure 5.2. A frequency response graph gives you a glimpse into the mic's sonic character.

Reading a frequency response graph is simple. The horizontal axis shows frequency, usually spanning the human hearing range (20Hz to 20kHz) with frequency increasing from left to right. The vertical axis shows output level from the microphone, usually calibrated in decibels. The mic's nominal output sits at 0dB; frequencies where the mic is more sensitive will push into the positive dB range, while less-sensitive frequencies will fall into the negative dB range.

A ruler-flat frequency response is not always the sign of a suitable mic. Humps and dips in a mic's response can be beneficial for recording certain instruments, as can a sloping response in either direction. Some handheld vocal mics have an upper-frequency boost, which is a nice complement to the mic's increased bass response due to proximity effect. This

often makes for a vocal sound that's both full and warm on the bottom end and crisp and articulate on the top (see Figure 5.3).

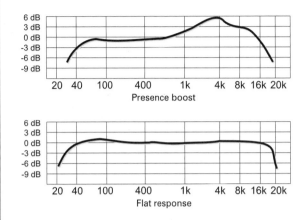

Presence boost

Flat response

Figure 5.3. Some handheld vocal mics (top) have a presence boost that's a nice complement to the increased bass of proximity effect. Compare this to mics with a flat response (bottom).

Because most sounds are a complex mix of different frequencies and amplitudes, small ripples in a mic's response aren't usually noticeable to the ear. Larger peaks or dips, on the order of several dB, are easier to hear. These irregularities in frequency response may be intentional, in order to make the mic a better choice for certain applications or instruments. These are usually designed into the mic by way of a special resonant chamber or cavity or by careful tuning of the diaphragm. Certain mics designed for bass drum or bass guitar recording don't have significant response past 10kHz. For the intended application, this limited frequency response is not a drawback at all (see Figure 5.4). Other low-frequency mics have a top-end response that extends to 16kHz and beyond.

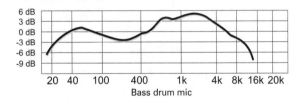

Bass drum mic

Figure 5.4. For certain specialty mics, a limited frequency response is not a drawback. This bass drum mic shows a frequency response tailored to its applications.

Sometimes, irregularities in frequency response are the result of an engineering compromise. Manufacturers use different methods and materials on inexpensive mics than they do on top-of-the-line models, with a corresponding difference in performance. No one expects a $75 dynamic mic to offer the smooth, extended frequency response of a $3,000 studio condenser.

Element type also plays a significant role in microphone frequency response. Though there are exceptions, condenser mics tend to deliver the flattest, broadest frequency response. Some condenser mics have a high-end response that approaches or exceeds 20kHz, and many have a low-frequency response that extends below 20Hz. Ribbon mics usually offer smooth, flat responses, though rarely with as much high- and low-frequency extension as the condenser. Dynamic mics tend to offer the most limited frequency response, with few dynamic designs pushing above 16kHz or below 50Hz. Depending on the voice or instrument and recording signal path, this frequency response may be more than adequate.

Some models offer the ability to alter their frequency response right on the body of the mic. Most common is a bass roll-off control—sometimes referred to as a highpass filter—which allows the high frequencies to pass through unaffected, reducing the mic's pickup of extremely low sounds. This makes the mic less prone to pop or pick up handling noise in live vocal applications. In the studio, bass roll-off can make the mic less sensitive to the rumble of an air conditioner or nearby traffic. Some mics offer several different bass roll-off settings, which usually change the point at which the mic begins rolling off bass frequencies. Some mics offer a choice of mild or steep bass cutoff filters (see Figure 5.5).

Figure 5.5. Bass roll-off selector. (Courtesy Shure Bros.)

Filters with steep roll-offs at low frequencies work well for eliminating mechanical rumble and handling noise and pops without dramatically affecting the mic's sound. Shallower slopes that start at higher frequencies are useful for reducing proximity effect in directional mics. These filters use similar techniques to solve different problems, and some mics offer both types of low-cut filtering.

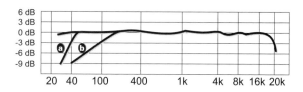

Figure 5.6. A steep bass roll-off (a) is useful for eliminating mechanical rumble without dramatically affecting the mic's sound. A higher, shallower roll-off (b) helps compensate for proximity effect.

Though not quite as common as bass roll-off controls, certain studio mics have a high-frequency roll-off switch or dial. Engaging this filter will help compensate for an overly harsh or brittle sound and will also reduce sibilance on vocals. On some instruments and voices, high-frequency roll-off will make for warmer-sounding recordings without the use of equalization.

Some mics offer switchable high-frequency boost as well. In the boosted positions, these mics capture a brighter, more detailed sound. Certain models offer several switch settings for electronically altering the mic's sound (see Figure 5.7).

Figure 5.7. Offering a high degree of control over frequency response right on the mic, the Electro-Voice RE38/ND has 16 different switch-selectable response curves. (Courtesy EV)

TRANSIENT RESPONSE

The next key performance characteristic of microphones is not one you'll find listed on a spec sheet. It has to do with how quickly a microphone's diaphragm responds to the "leading edge" of a sound. Called the transient, this initial impulse of energy is largely responsible for how crisp or sharp an instrument seems to the ear. Virtually every instrument, be it plucked acoustic guitar, snare drum or piano, has a transient spike at the onset of each note.

If the recording chain doesn't capture and preserve these transients, recordings will sound lifeless, lacking impact and realism.

The ability of a mic to respond to the transient of a sound is largely tied to its frequency response. Mics with an extended high-frequency response generally offer good transient response; those mics with poor top end are more sluggish. For this reason, we sometimes refer to the transient response of a microphone as its "speed." For those who slept through the section on inertia in high school physics, all this is related to the law that "an object at rest wants to stay at rest." Several design factors dictate how long a mic's diaphragm will stay at rest and resist the initial shove of a sound's transient (see Figure 5.8).

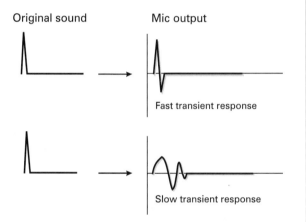

Figure 5.8. A mic with a fast transient response (top) will better reproduce the initial attack of a sound.

As covered in Chapter 2, the type of element a mic has plays a large role in its transient response. A dynamic mic generally has a relatively high-mass diaphragm assembly by nature of the thick diaphragm and coil of wire attached to it. Ribbon and condenser mics have much lighter diaphragms that respond more quickly to transients. Note that these are generalizations; not every ribbon mic, for example, has a very fast transient response. There's a broad range of transient response characteristics within each element type (see Figure 5.9).

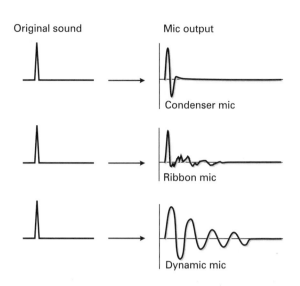

Figure 5.9. Condenser and ribbon mics generally offer fast transient response and little overshoot or ringing. Dynamic mics are slower to respond, and their more massive diaphragms continue to oscillate for an instant after the sound has passed.

For certain recording applications, condenser mics with small, ultra-low-mass diaphragms are popular (see Figure 5.10). These mics respond almost instantaneously to changes in air pressure, recording instruments with a high degree of realism and accuracy. While expensive mics are available that use this principle, many recordists have had great success with small, low-cost condenser mics designed for lavalier applications.

Figure 5.10. Condenser mics with ultra-small, low-mass diaphragms often capture recordings with a high degree of realism and accuracy. (Courtesy Earthworks)

Sometimes we refer to a mic's frequency and transient response as its "resolution." This term, which comes from the world of photography, sets up the best analogy for these aspects of a mic's performance. Certain subjects and applications (technical illustrations, for example) lend themselves to crisp, high-resolution photographs. For portraits or other artistic images, a smooth, soft-focus look may be most desirable.

In the same way, certain instruments, voices and musical styles work well when captured with a very detailed, high-resolution microphone. Others benefit from a softer, less-detailed recording. Just as a photographer applies lenses and filters to achieve the appropriate level of resolution, you can control the detail in your recordings with careful microphone selection. I'll explore matching the mic's transient response to the sound source in Chapter 6.

OFF-AXIS RESPONSE

When discussing directional mics, it's easy to concentrate exclusively on how they pick up sounds coming from directly in front of them. Manufacturers measure frequency response, sensitivity and dynamic range on-axis; only when a manufacturer prints a polar frequency response chart does off-axis sound pickup become an issue.

In reality, we live in an off-axis world. Sounds bombard a mic from all directions in most recording situations, either from instruments located to the side or from reverberant sound bouncing around a room. Since picking up some off-axis sound is inevitable, how a mic responds is important to the quality of the recording.

*In reality, we live in
an off-axis world.*

The very heart of a microphone—the element—is omnidirectional or bidirectional by nature. Designing a microphone to make this element more sensitive to sounds coming from a certain direction almost always has a negative effect on some aspect of a mic's performance. In most cases, the result is a directional mic that doesn't just make off-axis sounds quieter, but also changes their tonal character.

Perhaps the biggest compromise with off-axis pickup in directional mics is in frequency response. Because high-frequency sounds have much shorter wavelengths than low-frequency sounds (see Chapter 1), it's easier to control high-frequency directivity in a mic. Most directional mics offer a tight pattern at

higher frequencies and a rather loose pattern at lower frequencies. Some directional mics perform more like omnidirectional mics at bass frequencies, with little or no rejection of sounds coming from off-axis.

Manufacturers often print a polar response chart with a mic's specifications (see Figure 5.11). This chart shows the mic's sensitivity to several different frequencies at various angles around the mic. The further a given frequency line sits from the center of the chart, the more sensitive the mic is at that frequency and angle. By comparing the size and shape of the various frequency plots, you get a good picture of a mic's off-axis response. A mic with a perfect off-axis response would show an identical polar plot for all frequencies.

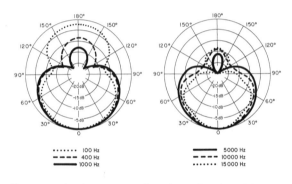

Figure 5.11. A polar response chart shows the mic's pickup pattern at various frequencies. (Courtesy Shure Bros.)

PROXIMITY EFFECT

Proximity effect becomes a factor when a directional mic is within about three feet of its sound source; the closer the mic is to the source, the more pronounced the bass boost. At extremely close distances (a few inches or less), proximity effect can generate an increase of over 10dB in bass frequency pickup. This boost decreases as frequency increases; proximity effect is much less noticeable in most mics above about 500Hz (see Figure 5.12).

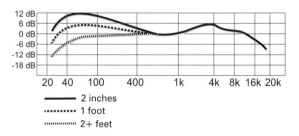

Figure 5.12. Proximity effect increases the bass response of directional mics when placed close to the sound source.

Proximity effect is most noticeable in bidirectional microphones, thanks to their purely pressure-gradient nature; cardioid mics usually exhibit slightly less proximity effect. With a few rare exceptions, most directional mics give some degree of bass boost due to proximity effect. Mic designers can minimize proximity effect with careful engineering. Some directional mic designs, especially those designed for extremely close miking of a speaking voice, have no proximity effect whatsoever.

MECHANICAL/HANDLING NOISE

Though less critical in studio recording than live sound situations, a mic's resistance to mechanical or handling noise is worth considering. While some mics can take a solid impact without making a sound, others will turn even the smallest bump into a loud noise. When an accidental touch to the pop filter or mic stand ruins an otherwise perfect vocal take, it becomes all too clear how sensitive some mics are to mechanical noise.

Most mics have some internal suspension to isolate the element from the mic body. Mics designed for live use often have heavy foam suspension; studio mics usually have much less isolation between element and case. Instead of damping vibrations and shocks internally, many large-diaphragm studio condenser mics rely on a special shock-mount basket that attaches to the mic stand. These mounts usually cradle the whole mic in rubber or elastic bands, greatly reducing any shocks carried through the stand (see Figure 5.13). The weak link in this system is often the mic cable itself. Since it attaches directly to the mic, it can transfer knocks or vibrations right through the shock-mount basket.

Dynamic and small-diaphragm condenser mics rarely have such elaborate external shock-mounts. These mics usually snap into a clip attached to the mic stand, making them more susceptible to mechanical noise transmitted through the stand. Although this can be a major problem in live sound or location recording applications, most studio recording involves stationary mics and instruments, so this may never be a problem.

Because most mechanical sounds are of relatively low frequency, they often show up in the recording as dull thumps. Engaging a bass roll-off filter will cut out most of the energy from these impacts, leaving a much less noticeable noise on the recording. Even if a mic remains cradled in its shock-mount for the duration of a recording, engaging the bass roll-off filter is a good idea if you suspect the mic may receive a jolt or bump.

Figure 5.13. A suspension basket protects the mic from mechanical shocks and bumps. (Courtesy BPM)

MAXIMUM SOUND PRESSURE LEVEL (SPL)

Like any mechanical or electronic device, a microphone has limits—such as how high or low a frequency it can pick up, how quiet a sound it can detect or how loud a sound it can accurately record. This latter characteristic is a mic's maximum sound pressure level, or max SPL. As an instrument or voice exceeds the maximum SPL of a mic, the mic can no longer record sound without adding increasing amounts of distortion.

Maximum SPL is a specification that many manufacturers measure and print in their literature. Measuring maximum SPL at 1% THD (total harmonic distortion) is common, though some manufacturers use distortion figures as low as 0.5% or as high as 3%. Specs usually show the maximum SPL in decibels, measured relative to the threshold of human hearing.

Sound becomes painful to the human ear as sound pressure levels approach 130dB; modern microphones commonly have maximum SPL ratings of 140dB and higher. Some condenser designs with attenuator engaged (more on this later) can cleanly record levels in excess of 160dB.

Sound can exceed a mic's SPL limit in two areas. The first is in the element itself. If sound causes the diaphragm or ribbon to move beyond its physical limits, it will no longer be able to track the changes in air pressure in linear fashion and audible distortion will result. With today's sturdy diaphragm designs, this is a rare occurrence. Sounds loud enough to cause severe distortion in a dynamic mic are not commonly encountered.

Likewise, it's not easy to drive a condenser mic's element into distortion. If a condenser mic is distorting, it's usually because the diaphragm's output has exceeded the headroom of the on-board preamp. This causes clipping in the electronics of the mic (see Figure 5.14).

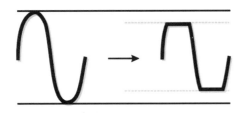

Figure 5.14. When a signal is too strong for an electrical component, the top and bottom extremes of the waveform are "clipped off" and distortion results.

Most ribbon mics will generate overload distortion at lower sound pressure levels than dynamic or condenser designs. Ribbons also tend to overload more easily at low frequencies. If a ribbon mic can handle a sound pressure level of 130dB at a frequency of 200Hz, it may distort at only 110dB when subjected to a 40Hz sound.

It's common for studio condenser microphones to offer an attenuator or pad for extremely high sound pressure levels. This switch reduces the effective SPL at the microphone, allowing it to record louder sounds without distortion (see Figure 5.15). Pads with 10dB of attenuation are common, while some mics offer both -10dB and -20dB settings. On a condenser mic, a pad reduces the diaphragm's output signal before it hits the mic's internal preamp. On some condenser mics with interchangeable capsules, the pad attaches onto the mic between body and capsule.

Figure 5.15. Some mics, like the Stedman SC3, offer two attenuator settings for high-SPL applications. (Courtesy Stedman)

SENSITIVITY

In Chapter 2, I discussed how a mic is a transducer, which converts one form of energy into another. Every transducer wastes some energy in the conversion process, and it's a simple matter to measure a transducer's efficiency by comparing its input to its output. In the case of a microphone, we can learn a lot about a mic by comparing its output voltage to the sound pressure level (input). We call this performance characteristic of a mic its sensitivity—the greater the mic's output signal for a given SPL, the more sensitive it is.

Sensitivity is an important performance characteristic, especially as it relates to unwanted electrical noise. In the world of electronics, it's impossible to boost a signal without adding in at least a small amount of random noise. In most cases, more signal boost (or gain) means more noise added. If a microphone has a very low sensitivity spec, it will put out a smaller signal for a given SPL than would a more sensitive mic. This smaller signal will require more gain before recording, usually resulting in higher noise levels. This weaker signal will also be more susceptible to RF (radio frequency) noises picked up in the cable or connectors.

The size of the diaphragm or ribbon is a significant factor in a mic's sensitivity.

All else being equal (magnet size/material, preamp design, etc.), the size of the diaphragm or ribbon can be a significant factor in a mic's sensitivity. Like a larger sail in the wind, bigger diaphragms generally offer a stronger output signal due to their increased surface area. In contrast, small diaphragms typically put out a smaller signal for a given sound pressure level.

The sensitivity of a condenser mic also depends on its internal preamp. Manufacturers can achieve almost any sensitivity figure with additional preamp gain, but the tradeoff comes in noise performance (we'll get into more detail on self-noise in the next section). A small-diaphragm condenser mic may offer similar sensitivity to that of a large-diaphragm model, but usually with an appreciably greater amount of self-noise. No amount of electronic trickery can sidestep the fact that the diaphragm or ribbon itself is the deciding factor in microphone sensitivity.

Perhaps more than any other mic specification, the sensitivity data printed by manufacturers can be confusing. The problem lies with the standard of measurement (or lack thereof)—there are at least four different and methods for measuring mic sensitivity. Because these methods use different reference points and units of measure (usually logarithmic), converting between them is not for the faint at heart. This complexity makes comparing mic sensitivity specs from different manufacturers almost impossible, except in the rare case where they use the same measurement methods.

SELF-NOISE

Placed in an environment completely devoid of sound, every microphone will still generate a certain amount of random noise at its output. In general, the more complex the electronic circuitry inside the mic, the more noise it will generate. Mics with no active internal electronics (dynamic and ribbon mics, for example) put out relatively small amounts of noise. Certain condenser mics, due to their active on-board preamps, generate enough noise to be clearly audible when recording quiet sounds.

Placed in an environment completely devoid of sound, every microphone will still generate a certain amount of random noise at its output.

Self-noise in condenser mics varies widely depending on the design and components used. Certain tube condenser mics exhibit high noise levels, though a tube design doesn't necessarily imply a noisy mic. Similarly, a solid-state condenser design doesn't always deliver low noise levels. The sensitivity of a condenser mic's element is a key factor in noise performance, as a highly sensitive diaphragm will require less noise-generating gain from the mic's on-board preamp.

Manufacturers measure and specify microphone self-noise in several ways. One is to state the sound pressure level that would generate the same output signal as the mic's self-noise. If a mic with an equivalent noise level spec of 20dB were in a room completely devoid of sound, the mic would generate a noise signal of the same strength as if there were 20dB of sound energy in the room. When comparing equivalent noise level specs, lower numbers mean less noise.

Another way manufacturers state self-noise is through the dynamic range spec. Dynamic range is the difference between the loudest sound the mic can record (max SPL) and its noise floor. Subtracting the mic's dynamic range from its max SPL will give you its self-noise. A mic with a dynamic range of 126dB and maximum SPL of 140dB, for example, has a 14dB equivalent noise spec (140dB - 126dB = 14dB).

Finally, manufacturers sometimes express a mic's self-noise spec as a signal-to-noise ratio. This ratio relates the mic's self-noise to a set value of 94dB SPL. Subtract the mic's signal-to-noise ratio spec from 94dB, and you'll have its self-noise figure. A mic with a signal-to-noise ratio of 70dB, for example, has a self-noise of 24dB (94dB - 70dB = 24dB).

When comparing microphone noise specs, there's one final factor to consider—the human ear. Our ears are most sensitive to noise at certain frequencies, whereas a normal noise performance test measures all frequencies equally. Hence a mic with a good noise specification on paper may put out more audible noise than one with a poor noise spec. Recognizing this, engineers came up with a "weighted" standard to more accurately measure real-world noise performance. Mics measured with this A-weighted scale show much lower noise figures, in accordance with what the ear would actually perceive. When you see "A-weighted" or an uppercase "A" tacked onto a dB spec (e.g., 18dBA), you'll know this scale is in use.

2

Microphone Techniques

Knowing how one mic differs from the next isn't enough to net you great recordings. You also need to know how to *apply* mics in real-world situations. This section will cover how to choose the best mic for a given instrument or voice, how many mics to use and how to position your mic(s) for the best possible recordings.

CHAPTER 6

Choosing a Microphone

How to pick the perfect mic for every recording.

Since the mic is solely responsible for the genesis of a sound, matching the mic to the instrument is one of the most crucial steps in the recording process. Professionals often spend a great deal of time searching out the perfect mic before recording a single note, sometimes auditioning dozens of microphones for each instrument or voice. While you may not have more than just a handful of microphones to try, it's still important to find the best mic for the application.

Picking the right mic involves a judgment call in most every aspect of mic design and performance: element type, pickup pattern, diaphragm size, maximum SPL, sensitivity, frequency response, overall tonal character and more. If this seems like a daunting list, don't despair; you'll soon become very familiar with all these characteristics for each mic you own. When you reach a point of familiarity with your mics, choosing which ones to try on a given voice or instrument will become second nature.

ELEMENT TYPE

How a microphone's element converts sound to electrical energy defines many aspects of a mic's performance. Deciding which element type is appropriate for a given instrument or voice is one of the first steps you'll take when choosing a mic. The decision will usually be between a condenser and a dynamic design, as the vast majority of microphones use one of these two element types. Some home studios may have access to ribbon mics as well.

Deciding which element type is appropriate for a given instrument or voice is one of the first steps you'll take when choosing a mic.

In general, condenser mics are highly regarded for their detailed, accurate sound. Condenser mics usually offer a broader frequency response than that of the dynamic. If your goal is the most true-to-life recording of a voice or instrument, the condenser mic will probably be your first choice. Keep in mind, however, that even condenser mics have their own characteristic sound.

Which isn't to say the dynamic mic has no use in the modern home studio; dynamic mics see daily use in studios across the world. When recording certain instruments, professionals often reach for $80 dynamic mics in lieu of $5,000 condenser models. Dynamic mics have become preferred by many engineers for recording electric guitar amps, drums and bass guitar cabinets. Certain vocalists, including some multi-platinum artists, sound better on a cheap dynamic mic than they do on an expensive condenser. It's also no accident that 99 percent of all vocalists use dynamic mics for live performance.

Transient response—how quickly the element responds to sound—varies considerably between condenser, ribbon and dynamic mics. Transient response times of the different element types can have a dramatic effect on the sound of some instruments. Sometimes a mic with a relatively slow transient response can be a benefit. Other times you want a mic that responds as quickly as possible. I'll explore the implications of a mic's transient response later in this chapter.

Beyond the differences in sound quality, there are a few practical considerations to bear in mind when choosing between dynamic, condenser and ribbon elements. The first is the condenser mic's on-board preamp. If a condenser mic doesn't have an on-board battery, it will require phantom power for this circuitry. If your mixer (or given mixer channel) doesn't offer phantom power, the decision is made for you.

Second, consider the amount of abuse a mic may experience during a session. Is there a chance a drummer will hit the mic with their sticks? Does a particular singer have a reputation for toppling mic stands? If ruggedness is going to be an issue, a dynamic mic will generally hold up much better. Though there are some rugged condenser and ribbon designs, you may want to think twice about using them where the mic may be struck, dropped or otherwise abused.

The final practical consideration is that of the recording conditions. If you're recording in a location with extremely high humidity or temperature, a dynamic or ribbon mic will usually offer more predictable performance. This is changing as manufacturers develop more stable condenser designs, but it's still a good idea to keep condenser mics (especially expensive ones) from environmental extremes.

Directional Pattern

A mic's directional pattern determines how it will respond to the sound source, the reverberant sound in the room and any other instruments or sounds that may be present. In practical terms, you can think of a mic's pickup pattern as representative of how focused that mic is. In cases where rejection of other sounds is important, a mic with a tight pattern is the best choice. Where rejection is less of a factor, looser pickup patterns (or even non-directional mics) may be appropriate.

CONTROLLING ROOM TONE

As sound waves bounce around in any enclosed space, the reverberant sound picks up the character of the room. This colored sound then becomes a permanent part of the recording, for better or worse. If the reverberant character of the room is flattering, then the room is a sound source you can use to enhance your recording. If the room sounds bad, you'll want to minimize its contribution to your recording.

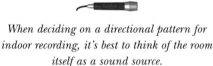

When deciding on a directional pattern for indoor recording, it's best to think of the room itself as a sound source.

Few home studios have the large, acoustically correct rooms that generate pleasing reverberation (see Figure 6.1). Small rooms, even those with sound treatment, tend to have sharp resonances that boost certain frequencies and reduce others. This causes an irregular response across the audible range, with certain frequencies reverberating much longer than others. If you record or overdub multiple instruments or voices in the same room, each will bear the character of the room. Added together at the mix, the acoustic "fingerprint" present on every track can taint the final result.

Figure 6.1. Because few home studios have the controlled, balanced acoustics of a professional facility, minimizing room sound is often a necessity. (Courtesy Shure)

For this reason, most home studio recordists should try to minimize the effects of the room on their recordings. The goal is to capture tracks that sound dry in isolation but are easily enhanced with artificial ambience at the mixdown stage. Choosing a mic with a tight directional pattern is one method for achieving this rejection of ambient sound. The other is to place an omnidirectional mic close to the sound source or instrument.

Engineers have quantified the amount of reflected sound picked up by the various directivity patterns, and the numbers are interesting to study. A cardioid mic will pick up roughly 60% of the ambient sound of an omni; a hypercardioid will pick up 50%. Translated to equivalent distances, these numbers tell us how far each pattern can be from the sound source and still pick up the same amount of ambience (see Figure 6.2). As I'll discuss in a moment, this does more than just make the ambience quieter; it affects the apparent closeness of the sound as well.

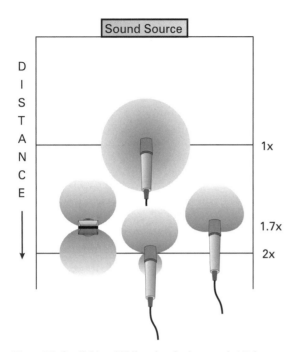

Sound Source

DISTANCE

1x

1.7x

2x

Figure 6.2. Cardioid and bidirectional mics can sit 1.7 times as far from the sound source as an omnidirectional mic and still pick up the same amount of ambience. A supercardioid mic can sit twice as far from the source.

If you have a room with uniform reverberation and no nasty resonances, it can add a great deal of natural spaciousness and depth to your recordings. One of the keys to capturing this desired room ambience is to use mics with broader pickup patterns. If you're using a variable-pattern mic with settings between cardioid and omnidirectional, experiment to fine-tune the amount of ambience recorded. Switching from a hypercardioid to standard cardioid, for example, will result in a greater pickup of room sound.

For maximum room sound, use an omnidirectional mic placed a good distance from your sound source. In addition to mics placed close to the sound source, try placing additional mics on the other side of the room to pick up room ambience. Pan the two mics in opposite directions to get a stereo effect, and blend these room mics in with the direct signal to get the desired amount of spaciousness. If you're recording in mono or are short on tracks, a single room mic will still add a noticeable amount of space to the sound. Keep in mind that most handheld vocal mics have a rising treble response. Used as room mics, these will often capture a very bright, unnatural ambience. You're better off using mics with flat frequency response characteristics.

APPARENT DISTANCE

The more directional a mic, the more it will emphasize sounds coming from directly in front of it; off-axis sounds and room ambience will be proportionally quieter. A hypercardioid mic will effectively block out much of the ambient sound in a room if placed close enough to the sound source, whereas, an omnidirectional mic will pick up the greatest amount of room sound. Because our brains decide whether a sound is close or distant largely by evaluating the ratio of direct to ambient (reverberant) sound, a mic's directional pattern affects our perception of how close the sound source is on playback. Placed the same distance from the sound source, a directional mic will make the sound appear much closer than an omni mic.

When you choose a mic for a given instrument or voice, consider the desired closeness (or front-to-back position) of the sound in the mix. Is it a sound that should hover in front of the speakers? If so, a highly directional mic will capture the least amount of ambience, giving the sound a very up-close character. If the sound should sit in the background, a less directional (or omnidirectional) mic will pick up more ambient sound from the room. This will make the brain perceive the sound as being further away from the plane of the speakers, moving it back in the mix (see Figure 6.3).

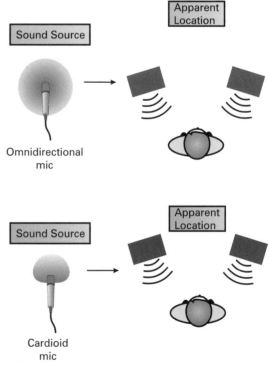

Sound Source — Apparent Location
Omnidirectional mic

Sound Source — Apparent Location
Cardioid mic

Figure 6.3. A directional mic will make the sound source appear closer to the listener than an omnidirectional mic at the same distance.

While it is possible to add electronic ambience to place a sound further back in the mix, this is rarely as natural-sounding as proper pattern selection and mic placement. It's not usually possible to remove excessive ambience once it's a part of the recorded sound. This makes it much harder to move a sound forward in the mix. For this reason, it's a good idea to err on the side of a tighter pickup pattern if you're not sure where a sound will sit in the final mix.

MULTIPLE INSTRUMENTS

There are times when you may wish to record more than one instrument with a single microphone. This can occur due to lack of microphones or because you wish to preserve the natural interaction of several musicians or vocalists around one mic. The number and type of instruments recorded affect the pickup pattern decision, as does the sound of the room itself.

If your recording space sounds good, you can use looser pickup patterns and greater distances between mic and instruments. If the room sound isn't great, or if you're trying to achieve a more up-front sound, you'll need to use tighter pickup patterns and closer miking. In some cases, the greater distances and looser patterns required to pick up multiple instruments or voices evenly make it impossible to fully eliminate room sound. If you need to record a large ensemble in a poor-sounding room, try dividing the group into smaller sections and recording them individually. This way, you'll be able to use tighter pickup patterns and closer mic placement for dramatically less room ambience.

We'll explore miking multiple sources further in Chapter 7.

Other Performance Factors

FREQUENCY RESPONSE

How a mic responds to different frequencies throughout the human hearing range is an important consideration when matching a mic to instrument or voice. Frequency response helps define the unique character of each mic, which can be dramatically different from one mic to the next. When we describe a mic as "dark," "bright" or "flat," we are referring primarily to frequency response.

There are two main aspects of frequency response that affect a mic's sound: breadth of response and smoothness of response. The breadth of a mic's frequency response depends on its upper and lower frequency limits. A perfect mic would be capable of picking up sound through the full 20Hz-20kHz range; in reality, few mics accomplish this.

The lower a mic's high-frequency response limit, the less clarity and air it will capture. A mic with a limited high-frequency response (rolling off at 10kHz, for example) will have a duller, darker sound than a mic that extends to 20kHz. Similarly, a mic that rolls off low frequencies below 100Hz will record less deep bass than a mic with a response down to 30Hz.

Like other limits of microphone performance, a narrow frequency response is not necessarily a bad thing. Matching a piercing, strident voice or shrill-sounding violin with a dark-sounding microphone, for example, may result in excellent recordings. A mic with a limited low-frequency response may help clean up the sound of a boomy, rumbly bass guitar cabinet. Mics with a very limited frequency response at both extremes may give you gritty, low-fidelity recordings, a sound that's growing more common in popular music.

Frequency response helps define the unique character of each mic.

Even more than the width of the frequency response, the smoothness of a mic's frequency response affects its sound character. Again, a perfect mic would respond to all sound evenly, without emphasizing or attenuating any specific frequencies. As with frequency response breadth, few mics achieve a truly flat response across the whole human hearing range.

The most predominant factor in defining a given mic's sound is the presence or absence of resonances. Resonances are specific frequencies where a mic's diaphragm, case or acoustic chambers actually store energy. After the sound has passed, the mic will continue to generate that frequency for a brief instant. Also called ringing or overshoot, resonances accentuate the mic's output over a band of frequencies. Resonances can be narrow or broad and can cause either a minor bump in frequency response or a pronounced spike. The severity, number and location of these resonances give a mic its unique sonic character or fingerprint.

A mic with numerous, sharp resonances will impart more coloration to the sound; a mic with little or no resonance will capture a more true-to-life, natural sound. Depending on the application and instrument, either can be appropriate. Less resonance is not necessarily better; engineers treasure some vintage mics for the unique coloration they bring to an instrument or voice. For example, the frequency response plot of a classic Neumann U47 looks like a design for a rollercoaster; yet it is one of the most sought-after vintage vocal microphones.

It doesn't take much deviation in frequency response to give a mic an unmistakable sonic character. If a mic has even a small peak at a specific frequency, that frequency may seem to dominate the mic's output. A peak of a few decibels in sensitivity around 1kHz, for example, can lend a midrange-heavy sound to a mic. A gentle rise in high-frequency response (above about 4kHz) often results in a bright, detailed sound. The broader the peak or dip in response, the greater effect it has on the sound. Narrow spikes or notches in a mic's sensitivity are rarely audible (see Figure 6.4).

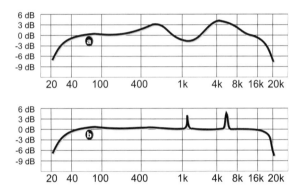

Figure 6.4. While broad peaks in frequency response will audibly color a mic's sound (a), narrower peaks are much less audible (b).

A word of caution: If you use the same mic for all your recording, consider the cumulative effects of that mic's frequency response. If the mic has a significant peak at some frequency, it will boost every sound recorded at that same frequency. In the final mix, all these peaks may combine to create a noticeable frequency emphasis. The less pronounced the sonic fingerprint of the mic, the less likely you are to experience this buildup of frequencies.

Learning the frequency response characteristics of your mics and how these affect their sound is a must for proper miking. Reading printed specs is helpful, but its no substitute for really listening to your mics. Experiment with your mics, comparing their sound on the same instrument or voice.

Listening to your mics is important because printed specs and frequency response charts can be deceiving. If a mic has a rising response at either end of its frequency range, it can sound brighter or bassier than a mic with a flatter response and broader overall frequency range. For example, Mic A has a stated frequency range of 30Hz to 19kHz, with a very flat response. Mic B has a frequency range of 30Hz to

16kHz, with a rise in its treble response above 6kHz. This rise (which peaks at +6dB around 12kHz) makes Mic B sound considerably brighter than Mic A, in spite of Mic A's broader top-end frequency response (see Figure 6.5). A similar thing will occur at low frequencies if a mic has a gentle rise or peak in its bass response. Put simply, frequency response specs can be deceiving.

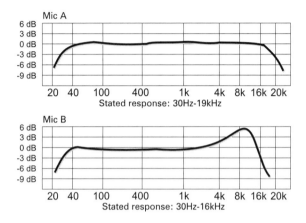

Figure 6.5. In spite of Mic A's better frequency response spec, Mic B will sound brighter due to its rising high-frequency response. Put simply, specs can be deceiving.

There's a sure-fire way to hear the resonances (if any) of several different mics. Set the mics up a foot or so from a vocalist, and have the vocalist sing a very breathy "aaaaaah" or "eeeeeee." Using the testing procedures detailed at the end of this chapter, listen for how the various mics color the breath noise. Specific frequencies will be noticeably louder on certain mics, seemingly changing the pitch of the noise as you switch from mic to mic. There's usually a resonance (or a series of them) where you hear the boosted frequencies. This test also works well with cymbals (crashed or rolled), provided you place the mics at least three feet from the cymbal for consistent sound.

TRANSIENT RESPONSE

As mentioned earlier in this chapter, transient response varies considerably between different element types. Even within element type, however, there's a good deal of variation in speed from one model to the next.

If your goal is to preserve as much of the attack transient of a sound as possible, a mic with a very fast transient response is a must. Recording the leading transient will preserve the crispness and detail of the sound. If you don't care about recording the attack transient (or if the sound doesn't have a sharp attack to begin with), transient response is not a factor. If you wish to avoid capturing the attack transient of a percussive sound, a slower response time is beneficial.

There are times when the attack transient of a sound can cause problems in the recording process. Consider the triangle struck by a metal object. The sound of the triangle begins with a loud, percussive "tink," after which it radiates a nearly perfect sine wave at a much lower level. A mic with a fast transient response will capture the sharp initial attack of the sound, passing it on to every other piece of gear in the signal chain. If gains aren't set correctly, this sharp spike of energy can cause clipping and distortion in the mic preamp, record amp, analog-to-digital converter or other components. When gains are set correctly to pass this transient without distortion, the sustain part of the triangle is recorded at a dramatically lower level than the transient. In a mix, the attack portion of the sound may be too loud while the sustain portion is too quiet (see Figure 6.6 [a]).

A mic with a slow transient response will not accurately capture the initial metallic attack of the triangle. Instead, the mic will reduce the intensity of the attack relative to the sustained portion of the sound. With the loudest part of the sound reduced in intensity, overall record levels can come up. This may cause the sustained portion of the sound to be as much as 10dB louder than when captured with a very fast mic (see Figure 6.6 [b]). The result is a stronger signal on tape or disk and a sound that will sit better in most mixes. Any sound with a very sharp attack transient can benefit by being recorded with a slow mic, be it acoustic guitar, xylophone or tom-tom. Even vocal sibilance will be less severe when captured with a slow mic.

We call this attenuation of the attack transient mic compression. Like electronic compression, a mic with a slow transient response will actually reduce the dynamic range of the sound source. Though transient response is intimately tied to frequency response, it's not a spec published by most manufacturers. You have to resort to other methods to discern the transient response. In most cases, it's easiest to compare the mic in question to a mic whose response you're familiar with. Virtually any small-diaphragm condenser mic offers extremely fast transient response and will make a good benchmark for testing.

Like electronic compression, a mic with a slow transient response will actually reduce the dynamic range of the sound source.

If you want to test the transient response of a given mic, there are several not-so-scientific methods you can use. Those recording to a computer-based hard disk system have it easy. Simply record the same highly percussive sound with both mics. Observe the first few milliseconds of each waveform, comparing the shape and size of the initial transient. The mic that has the most sharply defined, largest transient (relative to the sustained portion of the sound) has the fastest transient response. Normalizing both waveforms may make comparison easier; after normalizing, the faster of the two mics will have the smaller sustaining waveform.

If you're recording to a tape-based medium, you can often learn about the transient response by watching the meters. The faster the ballistics of the meters, the more accurately you can gauge the tran-

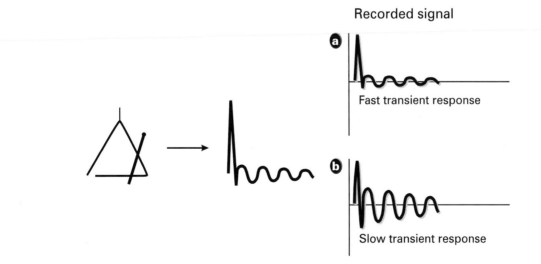

Recorded signal

a Fast transient response

b Slow transient response

Figure 6.6. Recorded with a "fast" mic, the percussive attack of a triangle may be much louder than the sustaining sound (a). A mic with a slower transient response will record a quieter attack and louder sustain (b).

sient response of the mic; for this reason, LED or LCD meters work best. Here's one way to test transient response with stereo digital meters: Point two mics at the same percussive sound source, setting input gains so that the sustain portion of the sound is at the same level for both mics. Pan one mic hard left and the other hard right, and watch the initial peak level for both. The mic that causes the meter to jump higher initially has the faster transient response. If the meters on your mixer or recorder are not fast enough to respond to the attack transient, a peak LED can alert you to the faster of the two mics. Note that these tests are far from scientific and are not a substitute for listening critically.

OFF-AXIS RESPONSE

As I discussed in Chapter 5, directional mics rarely maintain a perfectly even frequency response for all pickup angles. The off-axis response of a directional mic may be much darker than its on-axis pickup, or the off-axis frequency response could be riddled with sharp peaks and dips. Because every recording situation subjects a mic to at least some off-axis sound, how a mic responds can be an important factor in overall sound quality.

Using a mic that's less directional at lower frequencies can affect your recordings in two ways. First of all, the frequency response of the mic will change depending on the angle at which sound is hitting it. If a sound is appreciably off-axis, the mic may render it with a pronounced high-frequency roll-off. This makes sounds coming from off-axis darker as well as quieter. For this reason, proper positioning of a directional mic relative to a sound source is critical (see Figure 6.7).

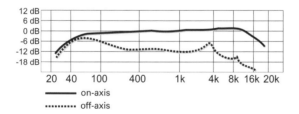

Figure 6.7. The off-axis frequency response of a directional mic often differs greatly from its on-axis response.

Second, the indiscriminate nature of directional mics at low frequencies affects the tonal balance of sounds you're trying to not pick up. If you've positioned a cardioid dynamic mic to point away from an unwanted sound, the mic still may pick up much of the low-frequency energy from that source. The result is a dull rumble of noise on an otherwise pristine track.

For example, consider an acoustic guitarist/vocalist miked with two cardioid mics. One mic points at his mouth, another points at the guitar. Sound from his voice is hitting the vocal mic on-axis and the guitar mic off-axis; the opposite is happening with sound from the guitar (see Figure 6.8). If the mics used have particularly uneven off-axis frequency response, the off-axis sound hitting each mic could result in a poor recording. If separation between voice and guitar is not a primary goal, a single cardioid mic (or even an omni) may offer a more natural sound.

Figure 6.8. Since most recording situations subject mics to off-axis sound, how much they color off-axis sound is an important variable.

Still, it's not often that irregularities in off-axis response make the directional mic a poor choice for recording. The ability to block out unwanted sounds (at least partially) usually outweighs the potential problems of the directional mic. Careful mic placement, especially with multiple sound sources in the same room, can go a long way towards alleviating irregularities in off-axis response. Finally, it's worth noting that better mic designs generally offer much more predictable off-axis responses. This is one area where engineering and design savvy make a real difference in mic performance.

PROXIMITY EFFECT

Proximity effect is largely a product of pickup pattern. Bidirectional and modified cardioid patterns have the most pronounced proximity effect, while omnidirectional mics generally have none. Remember that these are generalizations, however, and don't tell you the whole story. In reality, various mic designs exhibit dramatically different amounts of proximity effect, even within the same family of pickup patterns. One cardioid mic, for example, may give you little or no bass boost when further than four inches from the sound source. Another may pick up greatly exaggerated bass when placed 12 inches from the same source. Choosing a mic with the appropriate amount of proximity effect is important for capturing the best-possible sound.

Various mic designs exhibit dramatically different amounts of proximity effect, even within the same family of pickup patterns.

Proximity effect can be a help or a hindrance. You can use proximity effect to add fatness and punch to close-miked instruments, especially those that lack low-frequency power. Thin voices will sound richer and fuller as a result of proximity effect. Placing a directional mic close to a bass instrument will effectively extend that mic's low-frequency response, allowing it to better capture the lowest fundamentals of the instrument.

On the down side, proximity effect can accentuate bass frequencies enough to really sabotage a sound. Placed too close to an already bass-heavy instrument, a directional mic will make it sound even darker. Voices that lack clarity and edge will only get thicker if recorded close to a directional mic with strong proximity effect. Proximity effect also accentuates the popping of consonants such as "p" and "b."

Many handheld cardioid mics have a built-in high-frequency boost, which can help offset the dulling of proximity effect. This presence boost adds needed clarity to speech or singing, especially when the voice is miked from just a few inches away. When miking sounds at a distance of a few feet or more, however, this boost can make instruments sound thin and overly bright.

In addition to reducing handling noise or low-frequency rumble, the bass roll-off switch found on many studio mics can also help compensate for proximity effect. By experimenting with combinations of roll-off settings and distance between mic and sound source, you can often get a relatively flat frequency response from even close-miked sounds. Keep in mind that most bass roll-off filters affect only the lowest frequencies (usually below around 80-100Hz), and won't compensate for a build-up of mid-bass frequencies due to proximity effect.

HANDLING NOISE

In most cases, how well a mic resists mechanical or handling noises is not important in the studio. One notable exception to this rule is the singer that insists on holding onto the mic or mic stand during recording. This may happen because they're much more comfortable with the feel of a live performance, or they may be unable to keep from touching the mic expressively as they sing. A mic's resistance to bumps and knocks becomes crucial in this situation.

On rare occasions, a singer may want to track lead vocals in the control room, with speakers blaring, into a handheld mic. When this happens, you can usually write off any studio mic. Your best bet is to use a handheld mic with good mechanical noise resistance and hope it doesn't get jostled too much.

MAXIMUM SPL

When choosing a mic to record an extremely loud sound source, a deciding factor may be how well a mic handles high sound pressure levels. Certain mics are prone to overload at even moderately loud volumes, while others will withstand sound intensities far beyond what the human ear can tolerate.

While it seems improbable that a mic would experience sounds loud enough to cause distortion, such intense levels do exist in today's home studio. Close-miked drums (especially bass and snare drums) venture into these ultra-high SPL regions, as do powerful guitar amps and brass instruments. Often, an instrument that doesn't seem overly loud to the ear subjects a microphone to extremely high levels due to the proximity of the mic.

As you learned in Chapter 1, sound pressure level increases exponentially as you move closer to a sound source. Place a mic near the bell of a saxophone or inside a bass drum, and sound pressure levels can jump to 20 or 30dB higher than those heard from several feet away. Miked upclose, the human voice is capable of extremely high sound pressure levels. Driving a microphone into audible distortion is common for strong vocalists, and certain singers have gained a reputation for singing loud enough to actually damage fragile (and often expensive) studio condenser microphones.

It's important to recognize the tell-tale signs of a mic that's approaching its maximum SPL, as few mics add pleasing distortion to a sound when overloaded. Different mic designs exhibit overload in various ways. It's a good idea to learn the characteristic overload sound of your mics. In some condenser designs, the mic will begin to sputter and pop as sounds exceed its SPL limit. Some mics start sounding thin or compressed in response to overload; other mics lose their "air" and begin sounding darker than usual. Still other mics add a harsh, biting edge to the sound.

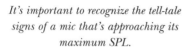

It's important to recognize the tell-tale signs of a mic that's approaching its maximum SPL.

There are several ways to compensate for a mic that's being pushed to the point of overload. The most obvious method (and most consistent for the recording) is to engage a pad if the mic has one. Unless volume levels increase dramatically after you engage the pad, this simple step should allow the session to go on. If the mic doesn't have a pad, moving it back from the source will lower the SPL. This can change the character of the recorded sound dramatically, especially in close-miked situations. The third option is to swap the mic for one with a higher SPL rating; this will virtually guarantee a noticeable change in sound quality. As a last resort, you can ask the musician to play softer or turn down the amp or ask a vocalist to sing with less intensity.

Because most of these solutions to an overloaded mic involve a noticeable shift in sound quality, it's a good idea to select mics that have plenty of headroom for the sound being recorded. Remember the tendency of musicians and vocalists to get louder as inspiration and passion hit. Start the session with a mic capable of handling this inevitable increase in level, instead of a mic that's already close to its SPL limit.

Few recordists have mic specs or an SPL meter handy when selecting mics; this makes it necessary to rely on the ear when deciding if a mic is suitable for a given instrument. The easiest test is to set up the mic in the position it will be in for the actual recording. Have the musician or vocalist give you their loudest possible sound (without hurting themselves or their instrument, of course). Set up gains to eliminate the possibility of any electronic clipping and listen closely for overload distortion from the mic. If the mic stays clean for this test, odds are it will not distort during the recording. If there's any hint of breakup, you should change the mic or engage a mic pad where available, especially if you suspect the musician or vocalist capable of even higher volumes. An old engineer's joke is that after completing the soundcheck (stage or studio), musicians always play 10dB louder, as soon as tape rolls or the audience applauds.

At the opposite end of the sound pressure level scale are the very quiet sounds, which can pose more of a challenge to a microphone and recording system than the loudest sounds. Whereas distortion is the enemy when trying to capture very loud sounds, minimizing noise is the main goal when recording those that are extremely quiet. As already mentioned in Chapter 5, the more sensitive a mic, the less gain its signal will require and the less noise will result.

Very quiet sounds can pose more of a challenge to a microphone and recording system than the loudest sounds.

Like picking a mic for a loud sound source, the guidelines for selecting a mic to record a quiet sound are simple: The quieter the sound source, the more sensitive a mic you need. For those unwilling to wade through the convoluted maze of sensitivity specifications, a direct comparison of several mics is the best method for gleaning which model is most sensitive.

Set up the mics you're testing the same distance from the sound source, grouping them as closely as is practical. Set all mics to a similar pickup pattern (if they're multi-pattern designs) and disable all built-in pads. Plug each mic's output into the same audio mixer or recorder, and bring up the mic preamp gains until all input channels are reading the same signal level (usually around 0dB). If the mixer's trim knobs have dB legends, you can get a reasonably accurate picture of how much gain each mic's signal requires to reach the same level. Inconsistencies in preamp calibration aside, the mic that requires the least amount of gain is the most sensitive.

You can compare the mic's gain knob setting to those of the other mics to quantify just how much more sensitive it is. If its knob reads -54dB, for example, while the others read closer to -60dB, the mic is roughly 6dB more sensitive than the other mics. A difference of even a few dB is significant and can make for a noticeable improvement in the noise level of the recording.

In most cases, a condenser mic will offer better sensitivity than any other element style due to the condenser's extremely light, compliant diaphragm. Some of the more expensive condenser designs offer both high sensitivity and high maximum sound pressure level. Many of these mics include a pad (as great as 20dB) to reduce the output of the sensitive diaphragm, extending their maximum SPL.

Mic sensitivity is less of an issue for normal to

loud sounds, as the strong sound pressure level virtually guarantees a healthy mic signal. For very loud sounds, an extremely sensitive mic is rarely the best choice. The resulting output signal may be too strong for the input stage of certain components, and the mic itself may be prone to overloading.

SELF-NOISE

Self-noise is another performance characteristic that becomes crucial when recording very quiet sounds. Like any electronic component at idle, a mic trickles out a small amount of noise even in a completely silent environment. This self-noise stays at a constant level regardless of the strength of the mic's output, becoming a permanent part of the mic signal.

If the mic is picking up a moderately loud sound, the mic's strong output signal will mask the noise and render it inaudible. If the sound is very quiet, however, the mic's self-noise will make up a much greater portion of the overall output. This signal will need considerable amplification before recording, a step

that will boost the mic's self-noise as well as the desired signal. The result is a hissy, noisy recording.

Because they contain no active electronics to generate random noise, dynamic and ribbon mics often have lower self-noise figures than condenser designs. This low-noise advantage, however, may be outweighed by the lower sensitivity of these passive models. For example, a given dynamic mic offers 6dB less noise and 8dB lower sensitivity than a condenser model. The recorded signal will still have 2dB more noise from the dynamic mic, as the additional 8dB of gain required more than makes up for the 6dB lower noise floor (-6dB + 8dB = 2dB).

As Figure 6.9 shows, a mic's self-noise and sensitivity interact to determine the amount of noise in the output signal. A very sensitive mic with a high self-noise output will generate a noisy signal, as will a mic with low self-noise and poor sensitivity. The best mics offer both low noise and high sensitivity, allowing them to deliver a noise-free signal from even the quietest sounds.

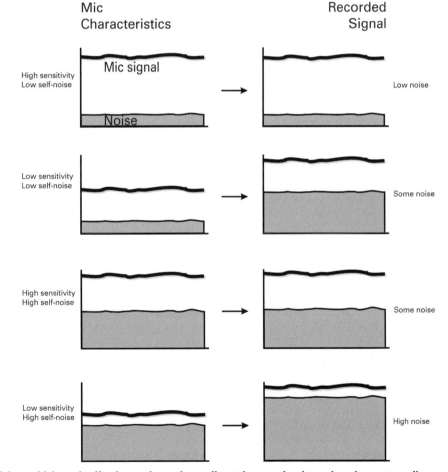

Figure 6.9. A mic's sensitivity and self-noise work together to dictate how much noise ends up in your recordings.

Mics come in a wide variety of shapes and sizes, from models 12 inches long and several inches in diameter to those the size of a pencil eraser. How you mount these mics and where you put them differs dramatically from one model to the next. Though most recordists would rather make decisions based on sonic quality, physical size and shape are sometimes the deciding factors when selecting a mic.

In rare cases, the size, shape or location of an instrument makes it difficult to get a large mic into the correct position. The instrument may be too close to a wall or gobo or some part of the instrument may keep a large mic from the best possible placement. Other times, the musician's playing style (a flailing drummer, for example) may dictate the use of small, unobtrusive mics.

Recording the modern drum kit is one application where mic size makes a definite difference. Getting full-size mics (and their stands) in and around existing drum and cymbal stands can be a difficult and time-consuming process. The best-sounding mic placement is often impossible to achieve due to these obstructions. Keeping mics safely out of the range of the drummer's sticks often dictates less-than-optimum placement for mics. For this reason, short mics with built-in swivel mounts or small mics that attach directly to the drum rim are growing in popularity. These mics—which may be of condenser or dynamic design—often deliver a drum sound every bit as good as that of larger mics (see Figure 6.10).

Figure 6.10. Small mics that clip directly to a drum's rim are growing in popularity due to their good sound and minimal space requirements. (Courtesy AKG Acoustics)

In the past, such small mics offered somewhat substandard sound quality. Today, smaller mics offer no-compromise sound, regardless of the instrument they're recording. Some engineers prefer smaller mics for their sound, even in places where larger mics would easily fit. Several companies offer a full range of small mics with a variety of frequency response characteristics and pickup patterns. Because they have such small diaphragms, these mics often exhibit a very crisp sound with extremely fast transient response.

Even when there's no space crunch, these small mics can come in handy. If a sax player can't stand still long enough to deliver consistent sound from a close mic, clipping a small mic to the instrument itself will give you a good recording regardless of their movement (see Figure 6.11). A similar approach would work for acoustic guitar, violin, flute and many other instruments. The small size of these mics also allows for more creative placement options when trying to obtain an unorthodox sound: miking a semi-hollowbody electric guitar from inside the body, for example, or an upright piano from under the lid.

Figure 6.11. If a musician can't stand still long enough to capture a consistent recording, attaching a mic directly to his or her instrument may be the best solution. (Courtesy Audio-Technica)

In rare cases, space considerations may dictate whether you use a side-address or axial design. There may be no room between floor tom and ride cymbal, for example, to put a long axial mic. A side-address mic placed perpendicular to the drum head may be a much better fit. You may run into similar space problems between an instrument and another mic stand or music stand or between another part of the instrument itself.

It's unfortunate that a mic's physical makeup and size sometimes take precedent over its sound quality in recording, and you may be tempted to do everything humanly possible to avoid such a situation. But before you try to salvage your mic placement at the musician's or vocalist's expense, consider a few things. First of all, the performer must be as comfortable as possible to perform at his or her best. A drummer may agree to change his cymbal layout for the sake of mic positioning, and the resulting sound may improve slightly. But if the new layout compromises his performance in any way, or undermines his confidence, the tradeoff was a poor one. It's always better to have a slightly compromised recording of a brilliant performance than a perfect recording of a ho-hum performance.

Second, your mic placement problem could turn into a sonic revelation. Being unable to use your tried-and-true setup will force you to experiment with different mics and innovative approaches to capturing an instrument. You may stumble across a great-sounding setup in the process, one you would have never tried if not faced with a miking dilemma. Some engineers purposely create such predicaments to force them to re-think their miking approach. They may leave their favorite mics in the closet or swap a condenser mic for a dynamic or vice versa for each instrument. If you're in a miking rut, try an experiment like this to get your creative juices flowing again.

Sound: The Whole Point

As folks who must constantly straddle the fence between technology and artistry, we have to be careful to not let one aspect dominate the other. Sometimes, when selecting a microphone for recording, it's easy to get caught up in the specifications game. When we do, we lose sight of the whole point of picking a mic: the sound. It's those unmeasurable performance aspects of the mic—its unique character and sound—that are most important in mic selection. When we rely on printed specs more than our ears, we rarely make the best decisions.

Getting the right mic in front of an instrument or voice may be the single most important thing you'll do in a given session. If you choose wisely, you'll capture a sound that will require little or no equalization or processing in the final mix. This offers a sonic reward (as after-the-fact processing can take a toll in sound quality) and makes mixing much easier. Make a poor miking decision and the sound will need a great deal of fixing in the final mix. Even the greatest outboard gear (to which few home studio owners have access) won't be able to make up for a poor mic choice.

Getting the right mic in front of an instrument or voice may be the single most important thing you'll do in a given session.

It's been said there are two approaches to recording: One is concerned with music reproduction and the other with music production. The first seeks to document a musical performance with as much accuracy as possible. Coloration of the sound is taboo, so engineers make mike selection and place-ment decisions based on the least possible coloration. Playback should sound exactly like the original performance, no better and no worse.

Sound production involves doing whatever it takes to get great sounds on tape. Music producers (note they're not called music "reproducers") pull out all the stops to achieve sounds that move the listener, regardless of whether they're an accurate representation of the original instrument or performance. If a highly accurate recording doesn't sound right, the producer sets out after a great-sounding *inaccurate* recording. Is this artistic heresy? No way. Most forms of art, commercial and otherwise, rely on creative alterations and interpretations of reality. Besides, what's natural about an electric guitar amp to begin with?

LISTEN UP!

Whether you're trying to capture a sound with clinical accuracy or maximum impact, the first step is to listen to the instrument or voice in the room. Get a good feel for its sound. Try to pinpoint the aspects you wish to accentuate or bring out. At the same time, listen for those qualities you wish to downplay in the recording. Is the sound too dark? Too thin? Too percussive? Just right? Ideally, the mic you choose will turn a deaf ear to those less-pleasing aspects of the sound, and bring the positive characteristics to the forefront.

Does a woman's voice have a breathy, wispy quality that you wish to accentuate? Choose a mic with a rising treble response to bring out these frequencies. Is a harmonica sounding thin and shrill? Try a mic with a less-sensitive upper-midrange response or one with a rising bass output. If faced with a dark-sounding instrument, a boosted presence response will add much-needed clarity and brightness.

Second, listen to how the instrument interacts with your recording room. Does the room reinforce the sound in a pleasing way or does the reverberant sound interfere with the instrument or voice? How much room sound you wish to record will affect your mic pickup pattern selection. To blend in a healthy amount of room sound, use a broad pickup pattern (or an omnidirectional mic). To minimize the effects of the room, choose a tighter supercardiod or hypercardioid design.

SHOOTOUT AT THE XLR CORRAL

At this point, based on your familiarity with the mics you own, you've probably narrowed your mic choice down to two or three different models. Now it's time to test the mics and decide which one is most appropriate. This takes a bit longer than just grabbing your favorite mic and starting to record immediately. It's worth taking the time, however, for two good reasons. First, you'll capture the best possible sound with the available mics. Second, you'll learn even more about the characteristics of your mics as you compare them on different instruments and voices. This shouldn't slow the session down much; once you decide which mic sounds best, you can quickly move the other mics and begin recording.

The procedure for comparing two or more mics seems obvious, but there are a few guidelines that will help you make the best decision. For starters, make sure you position the mics at an appropriate working distance from the sound you're recording. To insure they're all picking up the same sound, get them as close to each other as possible relative to the sound source. Be sure that one mic is not blocking or shadowing another in any way and that each diaphragm has a clear line of sight to the sound source. Set any pads or bass roll-off switches to the same position (usually off).

Because the ear tends to favor louder sounds, it's very important to set all gains so each mic input channel on your mixer is putting out the same signal level. This rarely means setting the gain control knobs themselves to the same position. Instead, route the mic inputs to a metered bus or stereo output. Mute all but one mic and set its gain so signal peaks are giving a strong signal without clipping (usually around 0dB). After muting the first mic and unmuting the second, set its input gain to match the level of the first mic. Repeat this procedure until all mics are at the same level. Set all faders to 0dB and center all pan knobs. Finally, make sure that all processing is disengaged for each channel, including equalization, compression, limiting and pitch-based effects.

Because the ear tends to favor louder sounds, it's very important to set all gains so each mic input channel on your mixer is putting out the same signal level.

Mute all mics but the first and have the musician or vocalist play or sing a brief phrase into it. Make a mental note of the mic's sound character. Mute that channel and unmute the second; have the musician or vocalist repeat the phrase into the second mic. Compare the sound of this mic to the first. Mute that channel and repeat the procedure for any remaining mics. If necessary, have the musician or vocalist adjust their position slightly to maintain the same angle and distance for each mic.

While auditioning mics, try to listen from the general to the specific. Which mic is giving the most pleasing overall sound? Which mic sounds the most natural? From there, listen for more specific characteristics. Is one mic brighter than the others? Darker? Fuller? Does one have tighter bass or less low-mids? Does one mic pick up more or less room ambience than the others? Based on your mental picture of the sound you're after, listen for those characteristics you wish to highlight or minimize. You may find it easier to concentrate on the sound if you close your eyes as you listen.

After listening to each mic several times, you should have a good idea which one is delivering the most appropriate sound. If you suspect that one of the mics may perform better at a different distance, move that mic and adjust its gain setting accordingly. As a final check, let the musician or vocalist improvise for several minutes. Have them give you a broad range of dynamics, tonal colors and pitches. Listen to each mic for a few seconds, switching rapidly between them. Use this time to confirm your impressions of the mics. When you've decided on the best-sounding mic, move the unused mics and stands to a safe place.

It's worth noting that this represents just one method of evaluating microphones. Any methodical approach will work just fine, provided you're careful to make the test as even-handed as possible. If you don't achieve consistency in mic placement, pad/roll-off switch positions or gain settings, you won't be able to make an accurate decision. Performing this test may take just a few minutes for a few mics or much longer if you're doing an exhaustive audition of many microphones. Professionals often spend hours on this step; you may not have that much time at your disposal. For a handy checklist to make auditioning mics easier, see Figure 6.12.

Mic Auditioning Checklist

Before beginning a listening comparison of microphones, make sure:

✔ Mics are at an appropriate distance from the instrument
✔ Capsules are as close together as possible
✔ Mics are not blocking each other
✔ Mics are pointed directly at sound source
✔ Pads are in the same position (off, unless needed)
✔ Boost or cut switches are in the same position (off, unless needed)
✔ Post-trim levels are equal
✔ Faders are at 0db
✔ Pans are at center
✔ Equalizers are flat or bypassed
✔ Compression or limiting is disengaged
✔ Effects are muted

Figure 6.12. Mic auditioning checklist.

CHAPTER 7

One Microphone, Many Microphones

When it comes to miking, there's often strength in numbers.

Up to this point, much of our discussion of microphone selection has assumed just one mic per voice or instrument. This one-to-one arrangement may be the most prevalent in modern recordings, but it's not the only way to capture great sound. Engineers commonly record a single sound source with several mics or several sources with a single mic. Knowing how many mics to use for a given application is as important as knowing which mic(s) to use.

The decision of how many mics to use depends on several factors. First is the sonic character you're hoping to record; certain types or genres of sound lend themselves to multiple mic techniques. The second factor is the specific instrument you're recording and whether you can capture it effectively with just one mic. Another important factor is deciding how the sound should sit in the mix. In most cases, you'll use a single mic to capture a discrete, focused sound that will occupy one specific area of the mix. Multiple mics are effective at capturing a broad stereo image or a spacious sound that seems to take up more room in the mix.

ONE MIC, MANY SOURCES

By now, you should have a good idea how to select a single mic to record a given voice or instrument. One mic is also an effective solution for recording multiple sound sources, provided you choose the appropriate mic and position it well. In this chapter, I'll

Solution: Move directional mic back

Problem: Uneven pickup

Solution: Use less directional mic

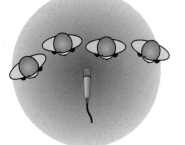

Figure 7.1. When recording many sound sources with a single mic, you may need to change mic distance or pickup pattern to get even coverage.

51

continue to focus on choosing mics; the next chapter will address microphone positioning.

In addition to the normal factors you weigh when choosing a mic for a single sound source, there are several other things you need to consider for miking multiple sound sources. These include the number, size and proximity of the sources; the sonic characteristics of the room; the presence of any unwanted sounds and the type of instruments (or voices) being recorded.

The biggest decision you'll make is that of pickup pattern. The goal is usually to record each sound with as true a frequency response as possible. This dictates that all sources be within the area(s) of greatest sensitivity of the mic. In other words, you want all sounds to be as much on-axis as possible. When sound sources are numerous, large or very spread out, this requires either a mic with a broad pickup pattern or a distant mic position, or both (see Figure 7.1).

If the reverberant sound and noise levels of your recording room are agreeable, you can select a pattern based solely on optimum pickup of the performers. An omnidirectional mic will give you true, uncolored sound from all the way around its perimeter, allowing you to arrange many performers in a circle around the mic (see Figure 7.2). Even with a large group of musicians or vocalists, each member will effectively be on-axis with this technique. An omnidirectional mic is not suitable if the recording space has poor-sounding (or excessive) reverb, as the mic will pick up a large amount of reflected sound. Likewise, an omni mic will not discriminate against any other sounds or instruments in the room.

A cardioid mic offers better rejection of room ambience and noise, but will only give an uncolored response over about a 130-degree angle. This makes the cardioid more appropriate for smaller ensembles, for groups of musicians you can place tightly together or for greater working distances between mic and musicians. The mic will record those musicians or vocalists that fall to the sides at a lower level than those directly on-axis. The mic's frequency response also grows less even for sounds positioned further off-axis.

Supercardioid and hypercardioid mics work fine for recording multiple sound sources, but offer progressively narrower working angles than the cardioid (see Figure 7.3). This makes these mics useful for recording just a few musicians or vocalists at normal miking distances (two to four feet). Proximity effect, which is more pronounced in super- and hypercardioid designs, should not be a problem at these distances. These mics offer good rejection of room reverberation and will discriminate effectively against unwanted noises or sounds if positioned correctly.

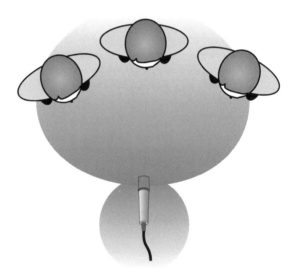

Figure 7.3. Supercardioid and hypercardioid mics are useful for recording two or three performers at a distance of a few feet.

The bidirectional pickup pattern is extremely useful for recording small numbers of instruments or voices. Placing a bidirectional mic directly between two groups gives you predictable, on-axis sound and good rejection of room ambience (see Figure 7.4). Remember that bidirectional mics have the highest degree of proximity effect, which may become a factor if you place sound sources close to the mic. In most cases, any more than four or five performers will be far enough from the mic to avoid appreciable proximity effect. The bidirectional mic also allows players or vocalists to see each other directly across

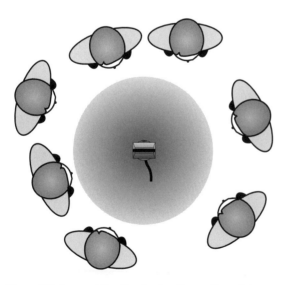

Figure 7.2. An omnidirectional mic allows all musicians or vocalists to be on-axis.

the mic, which can help them deliver their best performance. The null areas of the bidirectional pattern offer extremely good sound rejection, something you can capitalize on when trying to minimize pickup of sound from a certain direction.

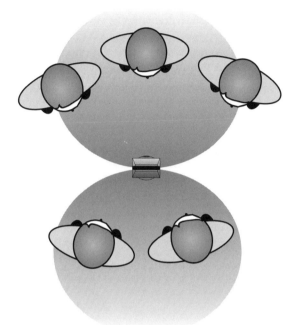

Figure 7.4. Positioning musicians or vocalists on both sides of a bidirectional mic is a great way to get clean, on-axis sound from mid-size ensembles.

Mics with multiple patterns between cardioid and omni allow you to experiment with looser directionality when recording multiple instruments or voices. This ability to use intermediate pickup patterns is a real help when a cardioid pattern is too tight for a given ensemble and an omni pattern picks up too much room ambience.

Multiple Mics

Though it increases the complexity of your recording setup, using multiple microphones is the only way to effectively record certain sounds. Using multiple mics on a single sound source allows you to create a stereo spread effect or add a sense of space and ambience around a sound. Using more than one mic on several sound sources allows you to minimize pickup of the room and gives you more control over the relative blend of the performers. You can also create a stereo image with multiple sources, either by using traditional stereo miking techniques or panning multiple mics through the stereo spectrum.

MULTIPLE MICS, ONE SOURCE

Though it may seem redundant to use more than one mic to record a single source, there are many instruments complex enough (or large enough) to benefit from multiple mics. For these instruments, each mic records a slightly different viewpoint of the sound. The grand piano is one example. It's common in pop music to record piano with two or more mics, each positioned in a different place on the instrument. Rotating speaker cabinets, with their spinning horns, almost always require two mics for even pickup and more if you want to create stereo effects as the horn(s) rotate from mic to mic. Other examples include vibes, percussion racks and drumkits; these usually need more than one mic for consistent pickup of the whole instrument.

There are many instruments complex enough (or large enough) to benefit from multiple mics.

Beyond the purely practical benefits, there are numerous aesthetic reasons for recording with multiple mics that apply even to instruments easily recorded with one mic. Perhaps the most common is to create a stereo image from an otherwise mono instrument. By placing mics in various positions around an instrument and panning them to different points in the stereo field, you can achieve a dramatic stereo effect. An acoustic guitar, for example, sounds great when recorded with a single mic. Properly recorded with two mics, though, it sounds larger than life. Both results are appropriate, depending on the desired effect. Even an instrument as small as an egg-sized shaker can pick up a noticeable stereo effect when recorded with multiple mics.

You can also use multiple mics to add a sense of space around a sound. This usually involves supplementing the close mic (or mics) with one or more ambient mics placed some distance away. Often called "room mics," these mics pick up reverberation from the recording space and delayed sound directly from the source. I'll discuss room mics more in Chapter 8.

You may also use multiple mics to combine the unique characters of two different models. In these situations, you place two mics (usually a dynamic and a condenser) in roughly the same position relative to the sound source (see Figure 7.5). Mix their outputs together in whatever proportion seems appropriate, usually combining the blend in mono and recording it to one track. Engineers often use this method for recording electric guitar amplifiers, placing both mics on the same driver in a single-speaker cabinet or each mic on its own driver for cabinets with multiple speakers. A similar approach will work for bass guitar cabinets as well.

Figure 7.5. Sometimes, combining the output of two different mic types can give you the perfect sound. Here, a condenser and dynamic design record a 4x10 guitar cabinet.

MULTIPLE MICS, MANY SOURCES

Finally, there are many recording situations where multiple sound sources are best recorded by more than one mic. You may use one mic per voice or instrument or break the musicians and vocalists into smaller groups and record each with one mic. Either way, the ultimate goal with multiple mics is control: control of independent levels, equalization and processing; control over isolation from unwanted sounds and noise; and control of room ambience. Though you eventually reach a point of diminishing returns, it's generally true that the more mics you use, the more control you'll have over the sound of your recordings.

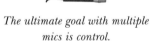

The ultimate goal with multiple mics is control.

Perhaps the greatest benefits of recording multiple sources with multiple mics are in the areas of levels and processing. With all sources sharing a single mic for uniform pickup, the only way to adjust relative volumes is to move individual musicians closer to or further from the mic. With multiple mics, you can change the level of each group independently before recording or at mixdown (if recorded to discrete tracks). You can also apply equalization or any dynamics-related processing (compression, expansion, gating) without affecting any other mic. Finally, you can apply time-based effects like reverb, chorus or delay in the appro-

priate amounts for each microphone.

Using multiple mics allows you to minimize the ambient effects of a poor-sounding room. Instead of all sound sources being a great distance from a single mic, multiple mics allow every musician or vocalist to be considerably closer to their particular microphone. This cuts down on reverb levels in two ways. First, the proximity to the mic dramatically raises the desired sound's level relative to the ambience. Second, miking smaller groups (or individuals) with discrete mics often allows the use of much tighter pickup patterns.

Recording a vocal quartet with four hypercardioid mics instead of one loose cardioid, for example, will cause a significant reduction in room ambience. In the same way, multiple mics will cut down dramatically on the level of unwanted noises (passing traffic, air conditioning, etc.) that find their way onto the recording. If you're trying to isolate one group of musicians or vocalists from another in the same room (rhythm section from vocalists, for example), multiple mics placed close to their sources will result in much less bleed (see Figure 7.6).

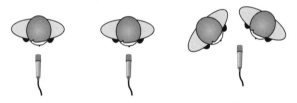

Figure 7.6. Dedicating a mic to each performer will cut down dramatically on bleed, ambient noise and room reverb.

There are drawbacks to using multiple mics, though. Getting mics very close to their sound sources can block out ambience too effectively. This kills the sound of the room and can result in a dry, sterile recording. Adding artificial reverb or early reflections will restore some sense of space to the recordings, but this is rarely as effective as capturing moderate doses of a good-sounding room. One solution is to put up a pair of room mics in addition to the multiple close mics (see Figure 7.7). This allows you to enjoy the greater degree of control from multiple mics while capturing a natural ambient sound.

Using multiple mics increases the amount of off-axis sound that ends up in your recording

Multiple mics can also result in a less coherent sound from an ensemble, often reducing the amount of perceived interaction among the musicians or vocalists. There's something almost magical about the sound of a group sharing a single mic, a phenomenon that may disappear when you split a group off onto individual mics. This lack of intimacy may be a product of closer mic placement or the loss of the shoulder-to-shoulder interaction of folks huddled around a mic. Whatever the reason, professionals often prefer to record even large groups in a good-sounding room with one or two mics.

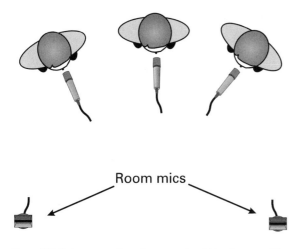

Room mics

Figure 7.7. Using room mics allows you to add back some of the ambience lost when close-miking musicians or vocalists.

The debate over few mics vs. many mics has raged in classical recording circles for decades. Some purists swear that the sound captured by just two or three mics is more cohesive and better represents the live concert experience. Others prefer the better-than-life sound of an orchestra or symphony miked with dozens of mics, each painstakingly processed and combined in a large mixing console. In reality, each recording approach has its unique merits. The final decision is based on personal taste.

As touched on in Chapter 1, multiple mics bring with them the potential for phase cancellation. As a given sound reaches several different mics at different distances, the inevitable delay causes certain frequencies to arrive out of phase. Where these notches in frequency response occur—and how severe they are—depends on mic placement, gain settings and mic design. As a general rule, more mics mean more potential for phase cancellation. Careful mic placement can go a long way towards reducing phase cancellation, as I'll explore in Chapter 8.

Finally, using multiple mics increases the amount of off-axis sound in your recording. With many sound sources in one room, there's a strong wash of sound moving in all directions. Every mic picks up a little bit of every source in the room, as well as what's directly on its pickup axis. Because these off-axis sounds often have colored frequency and phase responses, they can compromise the impact and clarity of your music when combined during recording or mixing. Like phase cancellation, the effects of off-axis sound pickup depend on the number of mics used, their placement and the relative volume of the various sound sources.

LESS IS MORE

There are no hard-and-fast rules for how many mics are appropriate for a given recording situation. The decision comes back to the experience of the engineer, as well as a firm knowledge of the mics available, the instrument(s) being recorded, the characteristics of the recording space and the desired sound. If that sounds like a lot to keep track of when considering the appropriate number of mics, it is. Selecting the right number of mics and positioning them properly is one of the most challenging aspects of recording.

Luckily, there are a few time-proven principles you can follow when deciding how many mics to use. The first is very simple: The fewer mics you can get away with, the better. For all the reasons listed in the previous section, a large number of mics can sound far worse than a few carefully selected, carefully positioned mics. If you can capture great sound from just two mics, don't use seven. When it comes to the number of mics used, less is often more.

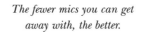

The fewer mics you can get away with, the better.

The second principle applies to all miking decisions, number of mics included. To quote legendary British producer Joe Meek, "If it sounds right, it *is* right." All the microphone theory in the world doesn't matter if it results in poor-sounding recordings. In the case of whether to use one mic or several, very few rules apply. The best approach is the one that gives you the best sound.

If you have enough microphones at your disposal, try setting up both close and distant mics at the same time. This usually involves a handful of mics placed close to individual instruments or vocalists, with a stereo pair positioned several feet away. Having all these mics up at one time allows you to switch quickly between multiple-mic and few-mic sounds. Before you decide on which approach best suits the recording, experiment with a blend of both. In many cases, a mix of both close and distant mics will offer the most pleasing sound.

CHAPTER 8

Microphone Placement

Picked your mic? Here's how to place it well.

When it comes to capturing the best recording of an instrument or voice, selecting the right microphone is only half the battle. The position of the mic relative to the sound source is every bit as important as the mic you choose. Position a great mic poorly and you're virtually guaranteed bad sound. Place a lesser mic in the perfect position and you'll probably end up with a workable recording. If your goal is to go beyond poor or even workable sound, you'll want to choose the perfect mic and place it in the best possible position.

Mic position makes such a dramatic difference in sound quality for many reasons, most of them tied to the physics of sound and the peculiarities of microphone design. Any one of these factors can cause dramatic changes in sound quality, even if you're moving a mic just a few inches from its original position. Finding the right mic position for a specific instrument or voice is largely a matter of trial and error, even for professionals with decades of experience.

Before I get into mic placement guidelines for specific instruments, let's explore some of the general principles of mic placement. These principles apply regardless of the type of instrument or music you're recording.

LEARNING TO LISTEN

Just as when choosing a mic (or mics) for a given instrument or voice, the simplest guideline of mic placement is to listen in the room. Get a feel for the character of the sound before you reach for a microphone. Walk around the room, listening for shifts in tonal balance and ambience levels. Where the instrument or voice sounds best to your ears is a great place to start experimenting with mic position. As I'll explore in the next section, every position of the room offers a slightly different aural perspective on the instrument.

The simplest guideline of mic placement is to listen in the room.

For close-miking, some engineers put one of their ears right near the instrument and plug the opposite ear. Listening for the sound that best matches what they're looking for, they try different positions all around the instrument. A mic will often end up in a standard location after this kind of test, but in-the-room listening sometimes prompts unusual and effective mic placement. Simply setting up a mic in the normal spot without listening rarely captures the best possible sound from an instrument.

This kind of critical listening takes practice to master; don't get discouraged if you can't hear significant differences in sound from one spot to the next right away. In time, your ears will pick up the subtle changes in tone from position to position. This new sensitivity will be helpful in every other facet of recording, as well.

INTERFERENCE PATTERNS

As sound bounces around in an enclosed space, there are areas where waves of sound reinforce and strengthen each other (constructive interference) and other areas where they cancel and attenuate (destructive interference). These "nodes" and "antinodes" fall in different locations for different frequencies, meaning the tonal balance of a given sound changes constantly from one position to the next. If the mic sits in an area where constructive interference is reinforcing a specific frequency, the resulting recording will have a buildup at that frequency. Likewise, the recording may exhibit a noticeable hole at a given frequency if the mic sits in an area of cancellation (see Figure 8.1).

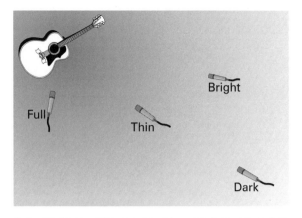

Figure 8.1. As sound bounces around a room, it creates pockets of reinforcement and cancellation at certain frequencies. Because of this, every spot in the room will have a different sound.

The location of these areas of reinforcement and interference depends on the size of the room, the position of the sound source and the wavelength of the sound. With wavelengths under an inch in length, pockets of boost and depression can occur extremely close together for the highest frequencies. Bass frequencies, with wavelengths of more than 20 feet, generally require greater amounts of mic movement for significant audible change to occur. Because of the way long wavelengths interact with any enclosed space (a phenomenon known as "standing waves"), most interference occurs at lower frequencies. High-frequency interference is most noticeable when a mic is picking up a strong reflected sound in addition to the direct sound. This can occur when a reflective surface (wall, window, music stand) sits in the vicinity of the sound source or microphone.

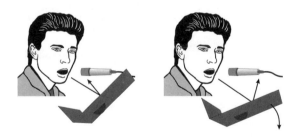

Figure 8.2. Even the humble music stand can cause reflections and audible phase cancellation. The solution? Angle the stand to bounce reflections away from the mic.

Believe it or not, reflections from the humble music stand can cause noticeable phase cancellation. Some people cover music stands with padded covers to reduce reflections. While this may help somewhat, it doesn't eliminate high-frequency reflections from the paper itself. A more effective solution is to simply

angle the stand to bounce reflections away from the mic. Usually this means placing the music stand as flat as possible (see Figure 8.2).

FROM A DISTANCE

Like a photographer deciding how far to place his camera from the subject, you have to decide whether you want to capture a close-up or a wide shot of your sound source. Moving a mic close to an instrument, especially a large one, allows the mic to focus in on just one aspect of the sound (see Figure 8.3). Positioned carefully, a close mic can emphasize the brightness, warmth, attack or sustain of a sound.

Positioned carefully, a close mic can emphasize the brightness, warmth, attack or sustain of a sound.

Figure 8.3. Up-close mic placement will tend to focus in on one aspect of the instrument's sound. More distant placement will capture the sound of the instrument as a whole. (Courtesy AKG Acoustics)

With more space between mic and instrument, you'll capture the sound of the whole instrument, not just one specific part. Air will also season the sound as it travels over greater distances, which is useful when you're trying to capture the most natural recordings possible. Almost like gentle compression, air will also partially absorb and reduce the intensity of leading-edge transients from highly percussive sounds. Close-miking, in contrast, tends to accentuate dynamics and transient peaks.

There are other factors in the mic-to-sound distance equation that make an unmistakable change in sound quality. The first is proximity effect. Within about two feet of the sound source, proximity effect can cause a low-frequency boost on the order of 10dB or more. By adjusting mic-to-subject distance, you can control the amount of low-frequency boost, much like low shelving EQ.

In most cases, there's an audible relationship between the distance from the mic(s) to the sound source and how close the sound appears to the listener. Understanding this relationship allows you to control the perceived front-to-back location of sounds in a mix by mic placement alone.

The human hearing system uses several auditory cues to discern how far it is from a sound source. Indoors, one of the main cues is the relative balance of direct sound and reflected sound. Sounds coming from nearby are a great deal louder than the accompanying reverberation due to the closeness of the sound source. Sounds traveling a greater distance lose considerable volume relative to the reflected sound (remember the inverse square law). We subconsciously interpret larger amounts of reverberation to mean that the sound is a greater distance away. The brain also evaluates the delay between the direct and reflected sounds. In general, the closer the sound is to the ear, the greater the delay.

Consider the difference in sound between someone whispering in your ear and someone shouting from the other end of a large room. The whisper will be nearly void of any reverberation, a sure-fire clue to the brain that the sound is very close. The shouts will be followed by stronger reverberation and reflected sound, even in a somewhat dead room. Substitute a microphone for the human ear and it will capture the same aural cues in the recording. On playback, the ear picks up these cues to discern the approximate distance between the mic and the sound source.

For a very up-front recording, one that seems to sit on the same plane as the speakers, use close mic placement. For a sound that sits further back behind the plane of the speakers, experiment with more distant mic placement (see Figure 8.4). Using a combination of close and distant mic placement for various instruments will create layers of depth in a recording. In addition to panning, equalization and effects, this can make for greater distinction and space between instruments. As you experiment with different mics and mic placement, remember that a mic's directional pattern has a large effect on the amount of ambience recorded (and the sound's perceived distance from the listener). See Chapter 6 for more information on pickup patterns and apparent distance.

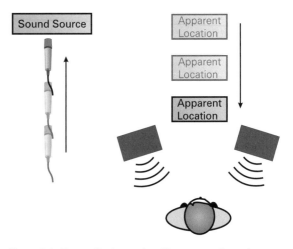

Figure 8.4. Close-miked sounds will seem to sit on the same plane as the speakers. Sounds miked from a distance will have more ambience, placing them further back in the soundfield.

While it is possible to change the amount of ambience around a given sound with effects, the end results are rarely as convincing to the ear as real-world reflections and ambience. For this reason, some engineers prefer to record and mix with no electronic ambience whatsoever. Instead, they rely entirely on the acoustic properties of the room and careful mic placement to create a sense of depth. This natural approach is more appropriate for some styles of music than others, though it requires a very good-sounding recording space.

OFF-AXIS ON PURPOSE

Directional mics give us more than just the ability to discriminate against unwanted sounds; they give us a great degree of control over the quality of the sounds we do want to capture. Most directional mics are more directional at midrange and treble frequencies than at bass frequencies. This results in a pickup pattern that changes in frequency response as well as sensitivity. On-axis, a directional mic usually offers the flattest response with the strongest high-frequency pickup. As a sound source moves further off-axis, high frequency pickup often becomes reduced and the sound grows darker (see Figure 8.5).

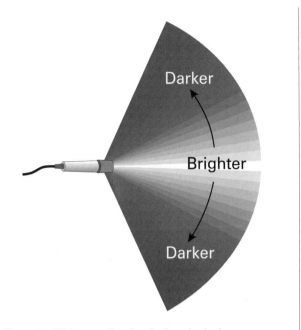

Figure 8.5. With most directional mics, the further you move off-axis, the darker the sound becomes.

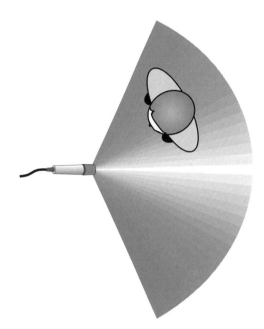

Figure 8.6. Off-axis mic placement will often give you a mellower sound, which may be perfect for certain voices and instruments.

close to and directly in front of an instrument or voice will pick up more upper harmonics, resulting in a much brighter sound.

Knowing this, you can position a voice or instrument slightly off-axis to control its tone. If you're recording an overly bright sound with a cardioid mic, for example, try positioning the sound 30 to 45 degrees (or more) off-axis. High-frequency pickup drops off somewhat at this position, which can make for a more pleasing sound (see Figure 8.6). The same technique often works well for vocalists with highly sibilant voices. A slightly off-axis position can reduce the strength of "s" and "t" consonants considerably.

A bidirectional mic will give you a similar degree of control. The sides regions of most bidirectional mics offer reduced high-frequency response, allowing you to position instruments or voices slightly off-axis for a darker sound. Bidirectional mics offer a very high degree of rejection at the sides; be careful not to position sounds too far off-axis or you could lose them completely. Also, as you angle a directional mic away from your sound source, be aware of what the mic is now pointing at. You may end up aiming the mic directly towards a sound source you don't want to record.

In addition to rotating the mic, you can rotate the instrument to change the recorded frequency balance. Most instruments, from voice to violin to acoustic guitar, radiate high frequencies strongly in just one direction. This high-frequency beam usually radiates out perpendicular to the instrument (see Figure 8.7). Since high frequencies are most directional, a mic not directly in-line with the instrument will capture a blend of harmonics heavier in the lower (less directional) frequencies. A mic positioned

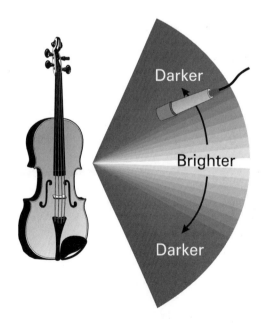

Figure 8.7. Most instruments radiate high frequencies in a relatively narrow beam. By positioning a mic off-axis with the instrument or voice, you can control the brightness of the resulting sound.

It's an unavoidable fact that the room itself is going to play some role in the sound of any indoor recording. You can minimize the room's influence by using a large amount of sound absorption, but this often results in a somewhat unnatural sound. Making the recording space as dead as possible has been a trend in past decades. Today, engineers generally prefer rooms with at least a small degree of ambience.

As I've mentioned in previous chapters, mic position and pickup pattern have a large effect on how much room ambience ends up in the final recording. A poor-sounding room generally forces you to use closer mic-to-source distances and tighter pickup patterns. Good-sounding rooms, on the other hand, allow you to pull mics back further from the sound source. This generally gives you a more natural sound with a better tonal balance.

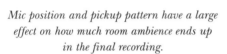

Mic position and pickup pattern have a large effect on how much room ambience ends up in the final recording.

With certain instruments and arrangements, you want the room to make a significant contribution to the recorded sound. In these cases, it's common to position mics specifically to record room ambience. Engineers usually mix these room mics in with the close-miked sound to add a greater sense of spaciousness and depth. The position of the room mics, though not as critical as that of the close mic(s), makes a difference in the quality of the recorded ambience.

It's most common to use two room mics, panning their output in opposite directions to create a wash of stereo ambience. You can also use a single room mic to add ambience to a sound, though it won't give the added stereo spread of two room mics. Room mics usually sit as far from the sound source as practical, often six or eight feet above the floor. When using omnidirectional room mics, which way they're pointing makes little difference. Directional room mics (not used as frequently as omnis) often point away from the sound source and toward a back wall or corner (see Figure 8.8). This minimizes pickup of direct sound, giving a little more control over the amount and character of the room tone without affecting the instrument or voice itself. If you have the tracks available, you can record these mics separate from the close mic(s). This allows you to add just the right amount of ambience at mixdown.

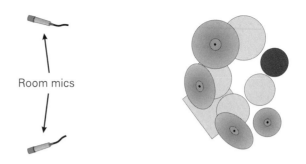

Figure 8.8. Room mics capture the natural reverberation and ambience of a room. Point directional room mics away from the sound source to pick up the smallest amount of direct sound.

When you wish to capture a sound with a strong room component but are short on mics, using just one or two mics several feet from the sound source will often give good results. In the case of directional mics, point them directly at the sound source. By changing the distance between mic and source, you can balance the amount of room ambience in the recording (see Figure 8.9). If you've got the mics at your disposal, try blending a close mic, a pair of more distant mics (several feet away) and a pair of room mics. If your room sounds good, you may be surprised at the rich sound that results. Remember, there are no hard-and-fast rules to room miking, so experiment with different combinations of close and distant mics.

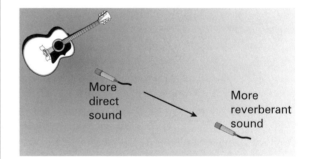

Figure 8.9. Placing a directional mic further from the sound source will pick up both direct and reverberant sounds. Adjust mic distance to control blend.

Multiple Instruments, One Mic

The amount of control mic position gives you over your sound is never more apparent than when recording multiple instruments or voices with a single mic. By using proximity effect, distance and pickup pattern to your advantage, you can capture excellent sound from diverse sources.

To review, mic-to-source distance has a significant impact on sound pressure level; doubling the distance between mic and instrument or voice creates a 6dB drop in signal level. If you're recording more than one sound source with a single mic, moving the individual sources toward or away from the mic allows you to control their relative level as effectively as with a mixer fader. Engineers use this technique frequently, adjusting the position of musicians or vocalists in increments as small as a few inches. In extreme cases, a very loud instrument may be several times as far from the mic as a quieter one being recorded with the same mic.

For example, say you're recording a small brass section of two trumpets and a trombone (see Figure 8.10). The first trumpet has the most important line of the section, so you position the player roughly four feet from the mic. The second trumpet and trombone parts should be at a slightly lower level than the first, so you place those musicians about six feet from the mic (a). When they begin playing, the second trumpet is much too loud and the trombone too quiet. You have the second trumpet player move back to roughly eight feet away and move the trombone player to the same distance as the first trumpet (b). The blend is better, but the first trumpet is now a touch too low relative to the other players. He takes a half-step in towards the mic, closing his distance to about three feet (c). This placement, combined with the players controlling their own dynamics, gives you the perfect blend.

This example illustrates several key techniques of mic placement. First, always use one player as a reference and keep him or her stationary. From there, move just one or two musicians or vocalists at a time. If you move every sound source at once, it can be difficult to find the best position. Second, if the blend is fine for all but your reference sound source, move him or her as a final step. Finally, mic and musician placement is helpful in achieving good balance, but the ability of the players or vocalists themselves is the greatest factor in a smooth blend.

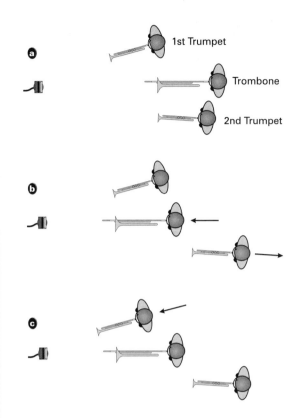

Figure 8.10. By carefully adjusting player distances from the mic, you can fine-tune their levels for a perfect blend.

As you position multiple sources relative to a single mic, remember that more distant sources are inevitably going to sound more distant. Unless you're recording in an extremely dead room, the sound of the more distant musician or vocalist will be bathed in a greater amount of room ambience. If you're trying to achieve different front-to-back placement of the various parts in the mix, you can use this "distant source = distant sound" relationship to your advantage. The main challenge comes if you're miking a quiet source and a loud source and want both to seem close to the listener. If you move the loud source back far enough to balance with the quieter source, it may sound too distant. In this case, you may need to record the sounds with separate mics (even onto separate tracks).

AMBIENCE

Once you get a workable blend between the instruments and musicians, you may move the mic to control the overall ambience level. While this will change the apparent front-to-back position of the recording, consider what happens to the relative distances from each instrument or voice to the mic. Move the mic back and the relative distances between mic and sources collapse. Move the mic in and they expand.

For example, say you've found mic-to-vocalist distances of two feet and four feet perfectly balance the levels of two singers. The more distant (louder) singer sounds roughly 6dB quieter than the close one. On playback, you decide you'd like to hear a bit more room ambience on the vocal track. You move the mic back so it's now four feet from the nearest vocalist. Now, though the room ambience is more prevalent, the further vocalist appears louder.

Here's why: With the mic two feet from the closest vocalist, you had a 2:1 (4':2') distance relationship between the two singers. At four feet, that relationship collapsed to 1.5:1 (6':4'), and the difference in level due to distance fell from about 6dB to roughly 3.5dB. One solution is to have the louder vocalist step back two feet to restore the 2:1 distance ratio (8':4'). Another solution is to restore the mic to its original position and add a room mic to pick up additional ambience. Finally, selecting a wider pickup pattern (assuming you're not already using an omnidirectional mic) will increase the pickup of room ambience without affecting the relative volume of the sources.

When recording multiple sources with one mic, you need to really know the proximity effect and frequency response characteristics of that mic.

Another factor in the distance equation is proximity effect. A bass increase can be a real benefit if your quietest sound is lacking fullness. But if one part of your ensemble is both quiet and dark in tone, you've got a problem: If you move the quiet sound closer to the directional mic for stronger pickup, the sound will only get darker.

Directional mics that have a presence boost or bass reduction to compensate for proximity effect give you one more thing to consider. With these mics, sound sources not in close proximity to them may sound thin. If your loudest sound (furthest from the mic) needs warmth to begin with, the directional mic's presence boost will make it even more strident.

Equalization is rarely the solution, as any tonal correction you apply will affect all sources recorded to the same degree. When recording multiple sources with one mic, you need to really know the proximity effect and frequency response characteristics of that mic.

Finally, pickup pattern gives you additional control over your sound when recording multiple sources. Positioning sounds relative to the directional axis of a mic helps you to balance out diverse sources in much the same way as changing their distance from the mic. For example, say you're recording two sounds with appreciably different levels but don't have enough room to move one source back from the mic. Using a directional mic, you can keep the quieter source on-axis and move the other one off-axis to better balance their levels. The further off-axis a source is, the quieter it becomes (see Figure 8.11). Eventually, moving the louder sound in 5- or 10-degree increments, you'll find a location that delivers more uniform levels between the two sounds. This technique will work with any directional mic, be it cardioid, tight cardioid or bidirectional.

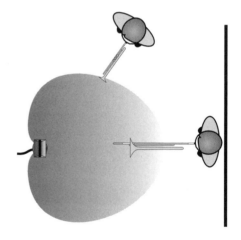

Figure 8.11. By moving louder sources off-axis from a directional mic, you can reduce their level without changing their distance. In this example, the trumpet will be roughly 4dB quieter than when on-axis.

It's important to remember the uneven off-axis frequency response of most directional mics when using this technique. As you place louder sources further off-axis, the odds of a noticeable tonal shift increase. Most directional mics, for example, have a reduced treble response off-axis. This makes for a darker sound when sources are located appreciably off-axis. As with proximity effect, you can use this to your advantage when miking multiple instruments or voices. Position the darkest sounds on-axis and move the brighter ones slightly off-axis for more uniform tone.

Sounds moved off-axis from a directional mic will also sound more distant than those on-axis because the mic will pick up a relatively consistent level of ambient sound regardless of where the source is in the room. If the source is on-axis, the direct signal is usually stronger than the room ambience. As the source moves further off-axis, the direct sound drops in level while the ambient sound stays constant. This makes for a more distant-sounding recording.

THE 3:1 RULE

Though using multiple mics gives you more options when recording, it can also create some problems. Phase cancellation, for example, becomes a greater concern as more mics populate a room. Since phase cancellation is greatest when the combined signals are of equal strength, lowering the intensity of one or more signals will greatly reduce cancellation. This is the principle behind the 3:1 rule.

The 3:1 rule says that with two mics picking up a single sound source, the distance between the mics should be at least three times the distance from the closest mic to the sound source (see Figure 8.12). Sound arriving at the distant mic will be considerably quieter than that arriving at the closer mic (thanks to the inverse square law), reducing the potential for phase cancellation. The distant mic will also be recording a more reverberant sound due to its position in the room, which can make phase cancellation less noticeable. If the two mics are closer together than the 3:1 rule dictates, their signals will be similar both in level and overall character. This accentuates unwanted phase cancellation.

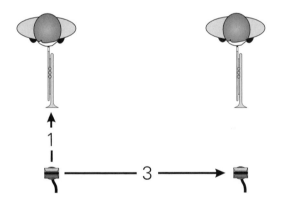

Figure 8.12. By observing the 3:1, rule you'll keep phase cancellation to a minimum.

Sometimes, out of necessity, you'll have two or more mics picking up the same sound source from roughly the same position. If objectionable phase cancellation occurs, try moving one mic in small increments relative to the other mic(s). Each position will shift the cancellation to a different set of frequencies. Eventually, you may find a position where the cancellation is less noticeable. The correct position for the mics is a matter of trial and error and depends in large part on the sound being recorded.

The 3:1 rule is more a strong suggestion than a universal mandate. Many popular recording methods place multiple mics at roughly the same distance from a sound source. Still, the 3:1 rule's main principle is worth understanding: Phase cancellation is less of a factor when multiple mics sit at significantly different distances from the sound source.

3

Blueprints for Miking Success

When it comes to putting a mic (or mics) in front of a musician or vocalist, there's no location that works every time. There are as many variations in mic placement as there are in instruments, music styles, recording rooms, engineers, etc. The keys to finding the right mic placement for *your* recordings are experimentation and careful listening.

Still, certain general mic positions have proven themselves effective over the years. These positions are a good starting point for your own mic placement experiments. Most of the time, you'll need to fine-tune the position somewhat for optimum recordings. Other times, these suggestions may result in very good sound with no adjustments.

In this section, we'll explore popular mic selections, placements and techniques for various instruments. Remember that these are *suggestions*, and may not give you the exact sound you're after. If getting great sound involved nothing more than following a diagram in a book, recording wouldn't be the rewarding challenge that it is.

CHAPTER 9

The Drum Set

Capturing killer drum sounds is easier than you might think.

The modern drum set is really a composite of a half-dozen or more individual instruments. Due to the sheer number of sound sources sitting just inches from one another, the drum set is one of the more challenging instruments to record well. Miking techniques vary wildly, depending on the style of music, the size of the kit and the number of mics available. At one extreme, some pop/rock engineers have the luxury of miking both sides of every drum.

It's good news for most home studio recordists that you can record a satisfying drum sound with just two or three mics. Even better (and more common) is a miking arrangement that uses between six and eight mics. In this section, we'll explore the full gamut of miking techniques starting with the simple and proceeding to the very complex. First, we'll split the drum set up and look at it on an instrument by instrument basis.

BASS DRUM

The sound of a bass drum (or kick drum) consists of an attack slap as the beater hits the head, followed by a deep fundamental tone. This fundamental tone is usually in the 50-150Hz range, though it may have subharmonics that extend well below the limits of human hearing. The sharp attack of the beater and the quickly decaying fundamental are the two elements that give the bass drum its characteristic sound. A drum sound with more fundamental than attack can sound dull and muddy, while a bass drum sound that's predominantly attack will be clicky and thin.

The composition of the beater makes a large difference in the sound of the bass drum. Felt beaters generally give a softer attack, while hard plastic or wooden beaters make for a sharper attack. Wood beaters wear out drum heads quicker, prompting some drummers to attach a small fiberglass disc to the head to protect it. This disc can further accentuate the attack of the beater, making the click too predominant for some musical styles.

The bass drum is capable of producing incredible amounts of sound at very low frequencies. The common practice of placing a kick mic inside the drum itself subjects the mic to intense sound pressure levels; delicate or very fragile mics need not apply.

Recording engineers commonly use large-diaphragm dynamic mics for bass drum for several reasons. Dynamic mics generally withstand extremely high sound pressure levels, and the slower transient response of the dynamic can make for a warmer, fuller sound. Large-diaphragm dynamics tend to capture the extremely low frequencies of the bass drum better than a small-diaphragm dynamic. Several manufacturers make mics specifically designed for bass drum recording or amplification (see Figure 9.1). On some bass drums, however, a standard small-diaphragm vocal dynamic works well. A cardioid or tighter pattern is common for bass drum, to minimize pickup of other drums and cymbals.

Figure 9.1. Large-diaphragm dynamic mics are a popular choice for bass drum recording, and many manufacturers offer mics specifically designed for bass drum. (Courtesy Audio-Technica)

Many condenser mics will withstand the high SPL of the bass drum to deliver excellent sound. Small or large-diaphragm models will work well; some engineers have great success with boundary mics placed on a pillow or blanket. Because of the intense SPL and large amount of air movement, ribbon mics are rarely a good choice for kick drum.

With a well-tuned and damped bass drum, the most balanced sound often comes from a mic placed inside the drum. This mic placement requires a front head with a sizable hole cut in it or no front head at all. A bass drum with both heads intact requires mic placement outside the drum, which can give you a softer, more pillowy sound.

Some engineers get good results by building a tunnel several feet long that extends out from the front of the drum, with the mic placed at the end. This gives the bass drum a different character due to the greater miking distance. Engineers often add a beater mic outside the back head of the drum to pick up a more crisp attack. The tunnel, usually made of chicken wire and packing blankets, involves more effort than most home studio recordists are willing to invest.

When miking a bass drum with just one mic, there are a few common positions to try. If the drum has a sizable hole in the front head (or no front head at all), start with the mic inside the drum. Place the mic perpendicular to the back head, about six inches from it, pointing directly at the spot where the beater strikes the head (see Figure 9.2). Increase this distance as needed; as the mic moves further from the back head, the attack component of the sound decreases. Placing the mic closer to the shell can change the sound dramatically, as can angling the mic away from the beater. If you don't have a mic stand, you may get good results from a mic laying on a blanket or pillow in the bottom of the drum.

Figure 9.2. Experiment with mic placement, distance and angle to achieve a good balance of beater click and head resonance.

Some drums sound best when captured by a mic that's a few inches outside the front head (see Figure 9.3). Point the mic at the beater and adjust its distance from the head as needed. This position will give a softer sound and will also pick up more bleed from the other drums and cymbals.

Figure 9.3. For a mellower sound, you may get good results by miking the bass drum from outside the front head.

Finally, you can try a miking position outside the back head of the drum, near where the beater strikes the head (see Figure 9.4). This position can pick up a lot of bleed from snare and hi-hat but may deliver the best sound with certain bass drums, especially in jazz recording. Place the mic a few inches from the head, angling towards the beater.

Figure 9.4. Some bass drums sound best when miked from near where the beater strikes the back head.

If you have the mics available, some bass drums sound best when recorded with two mics. One mic, usually placed inside the drum or near the front head, captures the fundamental tone of the drum. The other sits near the back head and captures the sound of the beater. You may need to flip the phase of one of the mics to avoid low-frequency cancellation or reduce lows from the beater mic with equalization.

Depending on the individual player's style, the snare drum can be the loudest instrument in the drum set. The sound of the snare drum consists of a sharp burst of high- and mid-frequency energy (from the snares themselves), accompanied by a quick-decaying fundamental tone. Most snare drums have a fundamental in the 80-200Hz range; the actual snares generate noise from several hundred Hertz on up to beyond the human hearing range. The top head of the snare generates most of the fundamental tone, while the bottom of the drum creates the bright snare sound.

Small-diaphragm dynamic mics are commonly used on snare, primarily for their ability to handle high sound pressure levels. The slower response of a dynamic mic (as compared to a condenser) adds a compressed quality to the sound, a desirable characteristic in many cases. At the same time, some drums benefit from the added crispness of a condenser mic. Directional mics, used for both added isolation and boosted low-mid response due to proximity effect, are the norm regardless of element type.

When miking a snare drum with just one mic, the conventional position is just above the rim, pointing in towards the top head at an angle (see Figure 9.5 [a]). The element of the mic usually sits just an inch or two above the top head. From this position, the mic picks up a very strong fundamental from the top head; you may need to apply some equalization to bring out the bright sound of the snares. In contrast, miking a snare drum only from below tends to make for an overly bright, brittle sound.

Mic position can make a significant difference in the drum's sound. Aiming the mic further down into the drum can cause it to pick up more bite from the snares. Greater distances from the head will reduce proximity effect and make for a thinner, brighter sound. As you position the mic, remember that the drummer needs unhindered access to the snare. Crowd the mic in too much, and it will inevitably get hit with a drumstick. This can spell the end of a mic or, at the very least, an otherwise perfect take.

Adding a second mic allows you to better capture the bottom head and snares. A dynamic mic will work fine for the bottom of the snare, though the more crisp response of a condenser may be preferable. Position is not all that crucial for the bottom head: A distance of 4 to 12 inches is usually fine. Point the mic directly at the bottom of the snare drum, being careful to aim the mic away from the hi-hat (see Figure 9.5 [b]). You will usually need to flip the phase of this bottom mic to avoid cancellation with the top mic. Experiment with distance and position to get the most pleasing bottom head sound.

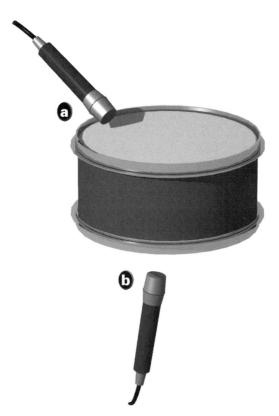

Figure 9.5. You'll often get the best snare sound by miking both the top and bottom heads.

TOMS

Toms have a more natural, sustaining drum sound than any other part of the modern kit. Following the crisp attack of the stick hitting the drum, most toms have a sustaining fundamental that rings out for several seconds. Toms with two heads have a more complex sustain portion, due to the interaction of the two heads. A good tom sound has a pleasing balance of stick attack and sustained fundamental.

The dynamic mic (small- or large-diaphragm) is a popular choice for toms for all the reasons listed in the snare section. In addition, the lower cost of the dynamic mic makes it a more affordable option when miking a large kit. Directional dynamics designed for vocal applications work very well on toms. Their proximity effect adds fullness and power, while the accompanying presence boost adds definition to the stick attack.

In most cases, a single mic positioned just above the rim will give excellent sound (see Figure 9.6). With the element positioned a few inches above the drum, point the mic towards the center of the head. Adjust the distance between mic and drum to control proximity effect and the resulting fullness of the sound. As with the snare drum, be careful to keep the mic out of the drummer's way. If the toms have no bottom head, you may get good sound from a mic positioned inside the drum itself (see Figure 9.7). If you need to capture two toms with a single mic, choose a relatively wide pattern and point the mic at an imaginary spot between the two heads (see Figure 9.8). In order to get good coverage of the toms, you may need to move the mic back further than when miking a single tom.

Figure 9.8. A single mic will usually do a good job recording two toms. Simply aim the mic at a point directly between them.

If you have the luxury of lots of mics and stands laying around, you could mic the bottom of the tom as well as the top. The bottom head will give you a strong fundamental tone, while the top head supplies the sharp attack of the stick. A directional dynamic or condenser mic placed a few inches from the bottom head should produce good results. It's a rare tom drum that sounds good when miked from the bottom head alone.

HI-HAT

The hi-hat is often the pulse of the drum set, driving the groove (or rhythm) forward. Like two small cymbals placed together, the hi-hat creates a sharp burst of mid- and high-frequency sound. For most musical styles, it's the very high frequencies from the hi-hat that you want to capture effectively.

For this reason, most small-diaphragm condenser mics work very well on hi-hat. The extended frequency response and fast transient response of the condenser allow it to record a very crisp, detailed sound. The less-articulate sound from a dynamic mic may be appropriate for certain songs or musical styles. Most engineers record hi-hat with a directional mic to help minimize pickup of other drums and cymbals.

A good starting point for mic placement is roughly six to eight inches above the hi-hat, pointing at the outermost edge of the cymbals (see Figure 9.9 [a]). The perimeter of the hi-hat tends to radiate the bright, characteristic sizzle we're usually looking to capture. Pointing the mic towards the innermost areas (near the bell) often picks up more of the hard tap of the stick hitting the cymbal. Placing a directional mic too close to the hi-hat can introduce proximity effect and accentuate this mid-frequency sound.

Figure 9.6. A directional dynamic mic just above the head of the tom usually delivers a crisp, full sound.

Figure 9.7. On toms with no bottom head, you may get the best sound by placing a mic inside the drum.

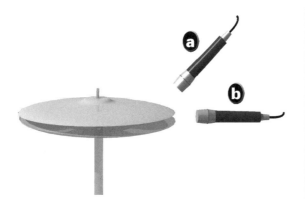

Figure 9.9. Placing the mic near the outer edges of the cymbals will capture the crisp, bright sound characteristic of the hi-hat. Keep the mic well clear of the blast of air that shoots out from the sides of the hi-hat.

As the drummer's foot closes the hi-hat, a blast of air shoots out from between the cymbals. If you put the mic directly to the side of the hi-hat, this rush of air can actually create a loud buffeting sound very similar to wind noise (see Figure 9.9 [b]). Positioning the mic anywhere above about 20 degrees from the horizontal should eliminate this problem.

Pointing the hi-hat mic carefully will cut down on the amount of snare and cymbals bleeding into it. Angle the mic away from the snare as much as possible without getting in the drummer's way. Because the snare is usually so much louder than the hi-hat, it can be virtually impossible to maintain isolation between them. If the hi-hat mic has a low-frequency roll-off switch, engaging it may help minimize pickup of toms, snare and bass drum.

CYMBALS

Like the hi-hat, cymbals tend to generate a great amount of mid- and high-frequency energy. This makes the condenser mic well suited to record cymbals. Large- and small-diaphragm condenser mics are frequently used as cymbal (or overhead) mics; both deliver excellent recordings.

Most drum sets have numerous cymbals, making it impractical to mic each one separately. The most common cymbal miking scheme is to place two mics above the drum set, panning them hard left and hard right for maximum stereo effect. A mic-to-cymbal distance of one to three feet works well, with closer positions offering slightly better rejection of other drums. Because cymbals also produce some low-mid rumble when struck, proximity effect can make for an overly dark cymbal sound when you place mics very close to them. Engaging the low-frequency roll-off switches will minimize this effect and also reduce the level of drums picked up by the mics.

There are two common overhead miking setups, both borrowed from traditional stereo miking techniques. The first places directional mics in a coincident-pair arrangement just above the drummer's head, with capsules as close together as possible (see Figure 9.10 [a]). This miking arrangement picks up a decent stereo image while maintaining mono compatibility (minimum phase cancellation when the stereo recording is played mono). As with any stereo miking, try to use two identically matched (or at least very similar) mics.

Figure 9.10. Two common stereo cymbal miking setups are the coincident pair (a) and spaced pair (b).

Known as the spaced-pair technique, the other miking setup spaces the directional or omnidirectional mics several feet apart over the left and right sides of the kit (see Figure 9.10 [b]). This can make for a much more dramatic stereo image, but with the possibility of phase cancellation if summed to mono. For maximum stereo separation, try placing the mics at the outer edges of the kit and quite close to the cymbals. Angle the mics outward slightly for better rejection (if directional). If the stereo image is too broad and middle cymbals are getting lost, try adding a third spot mic above and close to the center cymbals. Panned to the center, this mic will restore these cymbals (and the center image).

One Kit, Many Mics

Now that we've covered the instruments that make up the drum set, we're going to explore ways to get the best possible drum sound with the mics at your disposal. But before we begin, you should have a grasp of a key concept that applies to the drum set as well as every other instrument: The recorded sound of a drum set is a product of the acoustic sound of the instrument.

Nothing magical happens when you put mics around a drum set. If the kit sounds bad in the room, a dozen of the best mics money can buy won't make it sound good on tape. Likewise, a kit that sounds great in the room will sound great on tape, even if recorded with just two or three inexpensive mics. A poorly tuned kit with old heads, rattling hardware and a symphony of squeaks will thwart every effort to make it sound good, regardless of the talent of the engineer or the quality of the mics.

Assuming the drummer you're recording has a drum set that's up to the task of recording, here are some suggestions for miking the kit with any number of mics.

ONE MIC

Having to record a whole drum set with just one mic is usually a worst-case scenario, but you can do it in a pinch. Since a single mic won't give you control over individual drums or cymbals, mic position and the drummer's playing style are the key to capturing a good balance. Try miking the kit from a foot or two above the drummer's head (Figure 9.11 [a]) or from a few feet in front of the set (b). The mic's distance from the drum set will affect the amount of room ambience recorded, as will the mic's pickup pattern. The overhead position may also capture too much sound from the cymbals, depending on the drummer's playing style. For a tighter, more dry sound, use a cardioid or hypercardioid pattern. An omni pattern will pick up maximum room reverb.

To capture the full range and impact of the drums, a condenser mic should be your first choice. Any small- or large-diaphragm model with a flat, broad frequency response should deliver an accurate recording. A pressure-zone or boundary mic mounted to the ceiling, wall or floor will sometimes capture a very natural drum sound. Dynamic mics may not do the kit justice, especially those vocal dynamics with a presence peak or other compensation for proximity effect.

If you're after a small, low-fidelity sound, a dynamic mic with a very uneven frequency response may be perfect. To alter the sound further, try running the mic's output through bandpass filtering, heavy compression or even a guitar amp or other distortion source.

Figure 9.11. With one mic, try recording the kit from above the drummer's head (a) or a few feet in front of the kit (b). The latter position will often result in a more balanced sound.

TWO MICS

Adding a second mic will give you a shade more control over the drum sound, though two mics are far from the optimum miking setup. One approach uses a pair of condenser mics in a traditional overhead cymbal arrangement. This will give you a natural, distant-miked sound with the added benefit of stereo width. Large- or small-diaphragm condensers will work well; the more closely matched the better (see Figure 9.12 [a]). The main drawback is potentially overwhelming cymbals, depending on the drummer's playing style.

Figure 9.12. With two mics, try an overhead pair or single overhead mic plus one close mic.

Figure 9.13. With three mics, try an overhead pair plus a single close mic, or single overhead plus two close mics.

Another option with two mics is to supplement a condenser overhead mic with a single close mic (see Figure 9.12 [b]). This additional mic can be of condenser or dynamic design, though the latter is probably the most common. Using the techniques discussed in the previous section, place the additional mic on whichever drum needs the most reinforcement (usually the bass drum). Mix the close mic in with the overhead mic to add punch and energy to the recording.

Finally, you may try using a single overhead mic plus a semi-close mic in the vicinity of the snare, hi-hat and kick drum beater (Figure 9.12 [c]). By carefully adjusting position, angle and distance of the mic, you should be able to get a pleasing blend of these three key elements. The spot mic will capture a punchier, tighter sound while the overhead mic records a more spacious, reverberant sound.

THREE MICS

Adding a third mic grants you even more flexibility and control. Building on the previous mic setups, there are two effective ways to apply a third mic. The first is to supplement a stereo overhead pair with a close mic on the most needy drum (again, usually the bass drum; see Figure 9.13 [a]). This gives you nice stereo imaging and ambience coupled with the solid impact of the close-miked drum.

Another option is to use a single overhead with two close mics. Usually placed on kick and snare, these mics will give you good power and presence (see Figure 9.13 [b]). Try cheating the snare mic towards the hi-hat to reinforce it slightly. The main drawback of this setup is its lack of stereo imaging.

FOUR MICS

With four mics, the most effective setup is usually a stereo overhead pair plus two close mics (see Figure 9.14 [a]). With the latter mics on kick and snare (or kick and snare/hi-hat), you'll get strong impact plus nice stereo imaging from the cymbals and toms.

A variation on this setup close-mikes the kick and snare and moves one of the overhead mics near the hi-hat (see Figure 9.14 [b]). This mic reinforces the hi-hat while still capturing cymbals on that side of the set; the other overhead captures the opposite cymbals. You may need to narrow the panning of the overheads slightly to maintain stereo balance, but the additional reinforcement of the hi-hat can be well worth it.

Figure 9.14. With four mics, you'll get good sound from an overhead pair and close mic on snare and bass drum. Cheating one overhead outward will help reinforce the hi-hat.

With five or more mics, you are able to devote more microphones to specific parts of the drum kit (see Figure 9.15). A good starting arrangement is a pair of stereo overheads, dedicated kick and snare mics and an additional mic on hi-hat (a) or toms (b). In the case of a single tom mic, you'll get decent coverage of two rack or floor toms if you point the mic directly between them.

In a kit with two rack toms and a floor tom, try this five-mic setup: Close-mike the kick and snare, and place a third dynamic mic between the two rack toms. Cheat one overhead cymbal toward the hi-hat to give it greater presence in the mix. Place the other overhead mic roughly two feet from the kit, at a height midway between cymbals and floor tom (see Figure 9.16). This mic will capture cymbals while reinforcing the floor tom, making its sound more consistent with the two rack toms.

Figure 9.15. With five mics, you'll get good results from an overhead pair, close-miked bass drum and snare, and close-mic on hi-hat or rack toms.

Figure 9.16. With five mics, try spacing the overhead mics out further to pick up hi-hat and floor tom.

As the number of mics increases, you can begin close-miking more drums and cymbals in the kit. With six or seven mics, you need to decide whether it's most important to close-mike the hi-hat, close-mike each tom or add a second mic to the bottom head of the snare. You make this decision based on the musical style, as well as the sound and size of the drum set.

A selection of eight mics allows you to close-mike the kick, snare, hi-hat and three toms, in addition to the overhead mics. More mics means a bottom snare mic, a distant room mic or two and even a mic underneath each tom (see Figure 9.17). In the professional realm, it's not uncommon for engineers to use 15 or 16 mics for a large kit. If you have this many mics at your disposal, you're definitely in the minority of home studio owners.

Figure 9.17. With lots of mics and input channels at your disposal, you can mic nearly every part of the drum set (and both sides of some drums).

CHAPTER 10

Percussion

Sure-fire ways to round out the rhythm section in your recordings.

The percussion family boasts a great diversity of different instruments. Some are shaken or spun, some are struck with the hand, some are hit with mallets or sticks or struck together. I'll look at non-pitched percussion instruments first and progress to pitched percussion instruments later in this chapter.

Hand drums, such as congas, bongos, doumbeks and talking drums are relatively easy to record. Condenser or dynamic mics work well, though condensers usually capture a slightly more crisp, transparent sound. One cardioid mic will effectively pick up a pair of congas or bongos; try angling the mic down towards the heads from a distance of about 8 or 12 inches (see Figure 10.1 [a]). Proximity effect will emphasize low frequencies, something that may or may not be desirable. If the resulting sound is too dark, try moving the mic back in roughly two-inch increments or replace the cardioid mic with an omni. For more control and better rejection, try close-miking both drums with directional mics (see Figure 10.1 [b]). Though congas and bongos are usually quite close together, you may get some nice stereo spread by plac-

ing a coincident pair roughly six inches above the heads (see Figure 10.1 [c]).

Doumbeks and other large hand drums often put out a relatively low fundamental tone, one the proximity effect of close-miking will accentuate. Since these drums often develop their lowest sound some distance from the head itself, you may get good results with two mics. Place one near the head to get the crisp slap and a second mic further down on the drum to capture the deep fundamental (see Figure 10.2).

Timbales generate a very loud, bright sound with very sharp transients. A dynamic mic may compensate for this sometimes strident character and capture a warmer, fuller sound. A single directional or omni mic will usually pick up two drums effectively from roughly a foot away. If you use one mic for each drum, you can try closer placement for proximity effect.

Tambourine, shaker and cabasa have sharp, bright sounds well suited to recording with a small-diaphragm condenser mic. A dynamic mic will do a fair job, though it will often capture a darker, less crisp sound. Virtually any pickup pattern will work

Figure 10.1. Congas and bongos record well with a single close mic (a), two close mics (b) or a coincident pair (c).

well at mic-to-instrument distances ranging from a foot to several feet. Greater distances and looser patterns will pick up more room sound. A neat miking trick for shaker: Set up a spaced pair of mics roughly 8 to 12 inches apart and pan their outputs hard left and hard right. Have the percussionist move the shaker from left to right in front of the mics while playing. This will cause the shaker to smoothly pan from one speaker to the other (see Figure 10.3).

Figure 10.2. Some hand drums (like this doumbek) benefit from a two-mic approach.

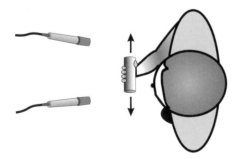

Figure 10.3. Moving smaller instruments between a spaced stereo pair of mics while playing creates nice panning effects.

Bell trees, chimes, triangles and finger cymbals put out the most delicate sounds of the percussion family. A small-diaphragm condenser will capture the extremely fast transients of these sounds and will do justice to the large amount of high-frequency energy they produce. Place the mic one to three feet from the instrument and select a pickup pattern based on how much room ambience you wish to capture. A stereo miking arrangement can make a beautiful wash of sound with bell trees and chimes. Try spacing a pair of cardioid or omni condensers about 12 inches apart, placing them 8 to 12 inches from the instrument (see Figure 10.4).

Figure 10.4. Miking a bell tree in stereo creates a wide, lush sound.

In the pitched percussion realm, vibes, xylophone and marimba sound great when recorded with a stereo mike setup. A spaced pair of mics placed one-third of the way in from each end works well, as does a coincident or near-coincident pair (see Figure 10.5). Start with the mics roughly 18 inches above the instrument and adjust distance as needed. Miking the instrument from below may give a somewhat darker sound.

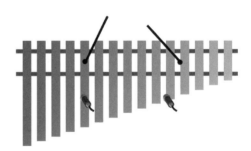

Figure 10.5. For tuned mallet instruments (like vibes), try placing a spaced pair one-third of the way in from each end.

Condenser mics are the first choice of most engineers for their crisp sound, but dynamic and ribbon mics will also work for these instruments.

Electric Guitar and Bass

Get maximum impact from electric guitar and bass
with these simple miking techniques.

ELECTRIC GUITAR

Perhaps more than any other acoustic instrument, the electric guitar's sound is as much a product of its amplification as it is the instrument itself. For this reason, the miking of an electric guitar is really a study in miking an electric guitar amplifier.

The most common mic used on guitar amps is a no-frills cardioid dynamic (see Figure 11.1). Because a guitar amp puts out neither extremely high frequencies nor fast transients, a condenser mic is of little benefit except for its often flatter overall response. The presence peak found in many directional dynamic mics seems to benefit most overdriven electric guitar tones and helps compensate for the proximity effect of close-miking. Still, many engineers get great results from small- and large-diaphragm condenser mics on guitar amps. With a condenser mic, experiment with different directional patterns and distances to control proximity effect.

Depending on the amp, room and guitar tone, you may find the best position anywhere from six feet to where the mic is touching the speaker grill or fabric. Within about two feet, proximity effect will begin to reinforce low frequencies. In many cases, one close mic and one several feet away will make for a pleasing blend of up-close sound and room ambience.

Large drivers (like a guitar amp's 10- or 12-inch variety) tend to beam higher frequencies in a very narrow cone straight in front of the speaker; lower frequencies radiate out in a broader pattern (see Figure 11.2). Because of this, mic placement even a few degrees off-axis can capture a considerably darker sound than directly on-axis. As most guitarists have their amps pointing at their ankles as they play, they're used to hearing an off-axis sound. The actual tone coming out of their speaker(s) may be much brighter than they realize, something they'll quickly discover when you place a mic directly on-axis. When miking an amp from a distance of a foot or more, you can position the mic off-axis to control the brightness of the guitar tone.

Figure 11.1. Because guitar amps put out high volumes over a relatively narrow frequency range, a dynamic mic is the first choice for many engineers. (Courtesy Electro-Voice)

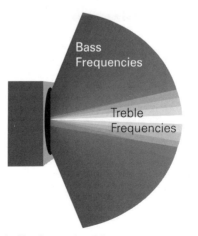

Figure 11.2. The larger the driver, the narrower its high-frequency pattern. Guitar and bass amp speakers tend to beam high frequencies in a very tight cone.

When close-miking a speaker, there's a similar technique you can use for passive tone control: placement of the mic on the speaker. Every point on a loudspeaker produces a different blend of frequencies depending on its distance from the very center of the driver (the voice coil). The closer you place the mic to the voice coil, the more high frequencies it will pick up. As you move towards the edge of the cone, high frequencies get progressively lower in level (see Figure 11.3 [a]). With some amps, close-miking at a point midway between the voice coil and speaker edge gives a good balance. Some amps benefit from the brighter pickup of a mic pointing directly at the voice coil. Finally, you can soften the close-miked sound of a guitar speaker by angling the mic away from the driver. This technique capitalizes on the darker (but often uneven) off-axis response of most directional mics (see Figure 11.3 [b]).

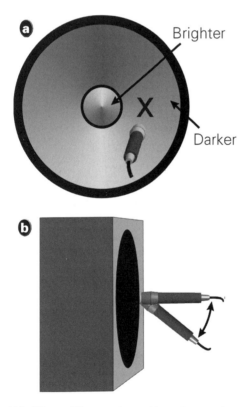

Figure 11.3. When miking a guitar cabinet, the sound gets brighter as the mic moves towards the center of the driver (a). A position midway between center and edge is a good place to start. You can achieve similar tonal control by adjusting the pickup angle of a directional mic (b).

When miking a cabinet with multiple drivers (such as a 2x12 or 4x10 cabinet), you need to close-mike just one driver. The sound from each driver is usually identical, making the potential for severe phase cancellation the only real benefit to close-miking multiple drivers. Some engineers do have success close-miking cabinets with one condenser and one dynamic mic, blending the two mics to achieve the desired sound. With this technique, you must take a great deal of care in positioning the two mics to avoid phase cancellation.

ELECTRIC BASS

Miking a bass cabinet is similar to miking a guitar cabinet, though the frequencies recorded are much lower. If you're getting the bass sound exclusively from the cabinet, you'll want a mic with an extended low-frequency response. Condenser mics will work well, as will any of the large-diaphragm dynamic mics designed for low-frequency instruments. Proximity effect from a directional mic can help you record a solid, deep bass sound.

You can combine the amplifier mic with a direct line from the bass, in which case the amplifier mic just adds character to the sound. Low-frequency pickup from the amp is rarely the main goal in this case, freeing you to use virtually any dynamic or condenser mic. Since you don't need the added bass boost of proximity effect when supplementing a direct line recording, you may get a more natural sound from a distant mic position (18 inches or more).

CHAPTER 12

Acoustic Guitar

Miking techniques for rich, crisp acoustic guitar sounds.

The acoustic guitar puts out a surprisingly broad range of frequencies, from under 100Hz to harmonics extending beyond the human hearing range. Low frequencies come from the resonance of the largest strings, while the plucking or picking action itself generates the shorter-lived high frequencies. Most sound radiates off the face of the guitar, with the soundhole contributing to the bass frequencies.

Figure 12.1. One of the most versatile mic positions for acoustic guitar is roughly 12 inches away, pointing at a spot midway between the soundhole and where the neck meets the body.

Over the years, engineers have established many common miking techniques for this popular instrument. Both condenser and dynamic mics will work on acoustic guitar, though the brightest, most detailed sound comes from the condenser mic. Both large- and small-diaphragm condensers will capture great sound from acoustic guitar. When picked hard, the acoustic guitar puts out a sharp transient considerably louder than the sustain portion of the waveform. This percussive sound may not record easily or sit well in the mix. Try recording picked acoustic guitar lines (such as leads) with a dynamic mic to reduce these transients for a more even, consistent sound.

Mic placement depends on the instrument itself, the recording space, whether the guitar is being picked or strummed and the musical style. Perhaps the most versatile placement for one mic is one to two feet from the guitar, pointing at a spot midway between the soundhole and where the neck meets the body (see Figure 12.1). With a directional mic, adjust distance to strike a balance between room ambience and proximity effect. With an omni mic, you should be able to place the mic closer and still achieve a balanced sound.

Placing a mic (especially a directional one) close to and directly in front of the soundhole often creates a dark, boomy sound. Likewise, placement further up the neck can produce a thin, tinny sound. The area around the bridge often produces a very strong upper-mid component, which may be objectionable on some guitars.

Other possible miking setups for acoustic guitar are too numerous to count. Sometimes the sound of a more distant mic is appropriate for the song and instrument. Some engineers have great luck miking the guitar from close to the player's head or even from behind the instrument. As with any aspect of recording, experimentation is key.

Stereo miking an acoustic guitar can effectively add space and apparent size to the instrument, especially on picked guitar parts. Directional or omnidirectional mics are appropriate for this application.

The most common miking setup is much like a spaced pair arrangement. It places one mic near the joint between the neck and body and the other closer to the bridge. Starting 8 to 12 inches away, try different distances between mics and guitar to achieve the sound you're after (see Figure 12.2 [a]). Another possibility is a spaced pair of mics roughly 12 inches apart, placed several feet from the guitar (Figure 12.2 [b]). This picks up a softer, more distant sound that may be more appropriate for a strummed part. Some engineers have captured pleasing guitar recordings with a M/S stereo miking arrangement a few feet from the guitar.

Figure 12.2. Close stereo miking of the acoustic guitar (a) can generate a larger-than-life sound. A distant spaced pair (b) usually results in a more natural recording.

Another way to use two mics to capture a fuller guitar sound is to place one close to the guitar and one more distant. The distant mic will pick up more reverb and room ambience, which can add space around the sound. This is only effective in rooms with a pleasing reverb tone.

Miking techniques similar to those used for acoustic guitar should deliver good results on classical (nylon string) guitar, dobro, banjo and mandolin. Condenser mics will best capture the silky air of classical guitar and mandolin, while dobro and banjo may benefit from the slower transient response of a dynamic mic.

CHAPTER 13

Piano

Whether grand or upright, here's how to get great acoustic piano sounds.

The piano presents several interesting challenges for recording, primarily due to its large physical size, broad frequency range and percussive sound. Pianos come in many different shapes and sizes, and no one miking technique will guarantee great results from every instrument.

Though some engineers regularly use six or more mics to record a single piano, you can usually capture a pleasing piano sound with one or two mics. Using two mics allows you to get a nice stereo effect from the piano, making it spread across the sound-stage as if the listener were sitting at the keyboard. A single mic will still pick up a nicely balanced sound, though without the stereo imaging. The sharp transients and complexity of the piano's sound make it a good application for either large- or small-diaphragm condenser mics.

GRAND PIANO

The brightest, most percussive grand piano sound comes from where the hammers strike the strings. This is a good place to mic a piano that has to cut through a pop or rock mix. A miking distance of several feet generally gives the piano a mellower, less percussive sound that's conducive to most jazz, instrumental or classical music.

For an aggressive piano sound, any of the stereo miking techniques will work when placed 8 to 18 inches above the hammers. A coincident pair centered above middle C will give good stereo imaging and excellent mono compatibility. Spacing directional or omnidirectional mics one to three feet apart over the hammers will give dramatic stereo imaging, as will a near-coincident pair (see Figure 13.1). You may find the optimum sound comes from greater distances between mics and hammers, either by moving the mics higher above the hammers or laterally down the strings.

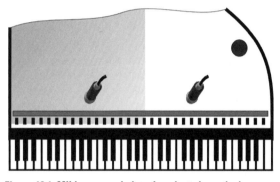

Figure 13.1. Miking a grand piano from just above the hammers gives a bright, percussive sound.

Mid-side (M/S) miking (explained in Chapter 21) is sometimes used on grand piano, though usually from a distance of several feet (see Figure 13.2). Such a setup won't give you a broad left-to-right spread across the keyboard, but it will give you a spacious sound. Many successful recordings have been made by combining a close stereo pair over the hammers and a distant M/S pair picking up the ambient sound of the room.

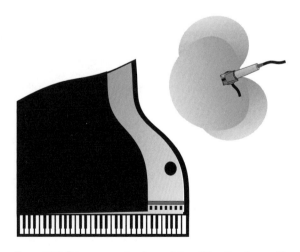

Figure 13.2. For a more natural sound, try miking the piano with a mid-side stereo setup from several feet away.

Experiment with other mic placements as well, including lower on the strings (especially over the bass strings) and under the soundboard. A combination of stereo mics over the hammers and other spot mics on the piano can be quite effective. Sometimes, you'll get an interesting sound by placing a mic near (or even inside) one of the holes in the piano soundboard. The pressure-zone mic can be very effective for recording the grand piano with the lid closed or at half-stick (see Figure 13.3).

When on the stick, the grand piano's lid reflects sound perpendicular to the sound board and out into the audience. These reflections can compromise your recording, creating phase cancellation whenever a miking scheme picks up a similar amount of both direct and reflected sound. For this reason, it's often preferable for recording to open the piano lid all the way or remove it altogether. If you can't do either, supporting the lid vertically is the next best option. Recording with the lid closed rarely gives optimum sound and should be kept as a last resort when trying to minimize other sounds bleeding into the piano mics.

UPRIGHT PIANO

The upright piano places the soundboard vertically and on the outside of the instrument, restricting access to the strings for miking. Hammers are usually near the top, and most uprights have a lid or panel that will open in that area. On some uprights, you can remove the surface directly in front of the player to expose the hammers. Try placing a stereo pair of mics in the area of the hammers, pointing them towards the strings. Though a coincident or near-coincident pair will work, you'll probably get the most dramatic stereo imaging by spacing the mics 18 inches to several feet apart. You can mount a pair of pressure-zone mics on the piano body directly across from the strings, depending on the internal layout of the piano. For a more cohesive sound, try suspending the mic(s) just above the player's head, pointing down towards the exposed hammers.

Upright pianos give you easy access to the soundboard, as it makes up the back of the instrument. Try miking the piano from the soundboard only or add a soundboard mic (or two) to a stereo pair on the strings. Since every spot on the piano soundboard radiates a unique set of frequencies, moving a mic just an inch or two can give a dramatically different sound when close-miking. For a more blended sound, try miking the upright from several feet off the soundboard. Any of the stereo miking setups will work, each lending a subtle stereo image to the recording. Miking the soundboard will give you rich tone with a minimal amount of attack; a bit of high-frequency equalization boost may help add definition to the sound.

Figure 13.3. A pressure-zone mic, mounted to the underside of the piano lid, will often capture a very natural piano sound.

CHAPTER 14

Electric Organ

How to best capture the earthy vibe of the electric organ.

For rock, pop, gospel and other styles, electric organ sounds are often as much a product of the rotating speaker cabinet as they are of the instrument itself. Usually called by its trademark name (Leslie cabinet), this speaker has at least one rotating horn that creates a swirling, vibrato/tremolo sound. In most rotating speaker systems, the player controls the speed of the rotating speaker(s) by toggling between a slow speed (or stationary position) and a fast speed. Combined with numerous drawbar settings and volume-dependent overdrive, the rotating speaker gives the organist a diverse range of tones to choose from.

The rotating speaker cabinet is a two-way system, consisting of a high-frequency horn and low-frequency driver (which may also sit in a rotating horn assembly). Though the limited high-frequency output of the rotating speaker cabinet makes it a good match for most any type of mic, engineers commonly use small-diaphragm condensers for recording the treble horn. A mic with a solid, extended low-frequency response works well for the bass driver. A large-diaphragm dynamic mic frequently gets the nod for this application.

Unless miking the cabinet from several feet away, you'll need at least two mics to capture a good tonal balance. You'll get the most impressive results if you record the rotating speaker cabinet in stereo with two mics to capture a broad wash of sound. Use another mic to pick up the bass driver or two additional mics if the cabinet has a rotating bass assembly.

For the treble horn, try placing two directional mics at the outer edges of the speaker's face. Point these mics at the center of the speaker's arc, being careful to offset the mics for speaker horns not centered behind the grill (see Figure 14.1 [a]). Panned into opposite speakers, this mic placement will deliver dramatic, spacious stereo. For rotating bass horns, use a similar placement for the low-frequency mics. A variation on this placement scheme puts mics on adjacent sides of the cabinet, pointing in to the center of each horn's arc (Figure 14.1 [b]). These miking arrangements capture a very up-close, crisp sound.

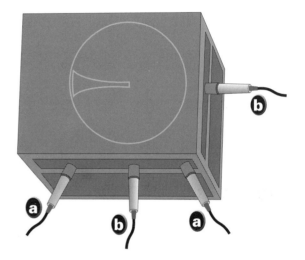

Figure 14.1. A rotating speaker cabinet will generate broad stereo effects if miked properly. For mono recording, place a single mic several feet away for a balanced sound.

For a more ambiguous, diffused sound, try miking the rotating speaker cabinet from a distance of several feet (even as much as 20 feet). A single mic at a greater distance will capture a cohesive, balanced sound from the cabinet. Using a stereo pair at a distance of 6 to 10 feet will still deliver a cohesive sound with the benefit of some subtle stereo imaging. Avoid mics with strong presence peaks, as these will often result in a thin, overly bright sound.

CHAPTER 15

Harmonica and Accordion

Great-sounding miking techniques for those other reed instruments.

The harmonica is capable of an extremely broad range of dynamics and tonal colors. Its strong midrange component and limited frequency range makes it an easy task for almost any microphone.

There are three common techniques for miking harmonica, and the style of music often dictates which to use. For folk, pop and other musical styles needing a very natural harmonica sound, try miking the harmonica from one foot to several feet away (see

denser mic only for distant miking; the moisture coming off the back of a harmonica could ruin a condenser mic.

Finally, some harmonica players run the output of their mic through a guitar amp. They usually set the amp to overdrive as they play louder, giving the harmonica the characteristic edge of a blues harp. For recording, simply set up your mic as you would for an electric guitar amp (Figure 15.1 [c]).

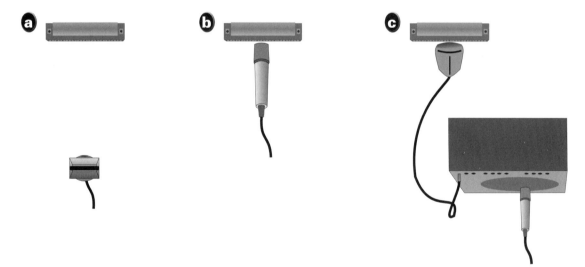

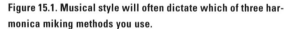

Figure 15.1 [a]). A condenser mic will usually capture the most natural-sounding performance, though a dynamic mic may be more appropriate in some cases. If the harmonica sounds too thin with a distant mic, try moving a directional mic closer to the instrument for some proximity effect bass boost.

Some harmonica players hold a dynamic mic directly against the harmonica by cupping it in their hands (Figure 15.1 [b]). This captures a very colored sound that's characteristic of blues and rock musical styles. Players that use this technique will usually have a favorite mic for this purpose, often a bullet-style mic designed for harmonica. If they don't have a mic preference, start with a cardioid dynamic vocal mic. The proximity effect and presence peak of these mics are usually key components of the sound. Use a con-

Figure 15.1. Musical style will often dictate which of three harmonica miking methods you use.

There are two techniques you can try to get a different amped harmonica sound. The first is to tap into the mic signal before it gets to the amp and mix a small amount of the resulting clean sound with the overdriven sound. Second, with the harmonica player in the same room as his or her close-miked amp, put up a room mic several feet from the amp. Position the player near the room mic. By changing the player's position, you can achieve an interesting blend of close-miked amp, amp room mic and natural harmonic sound. Try panning the two mics left and right for a spacious stereo effect.

ACCORDION

The accordion emits its lowest notes from one side of the instrument and its highest notes from the other. Positioning one mic at each side of the instrument will often pick up the best accordion sound, with the added benefit of some nice stereo imaging (see Figure 15.2 [a]). You can get a nicely balanced accordion sound with one mic, provided it's at least two or three feet from the instrument (Figure 15.2 [b]).

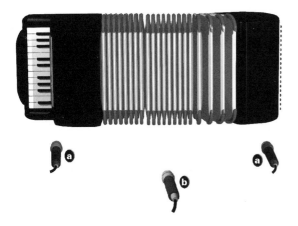

Figure 15.2. The accordion puts out high tones from one side and bass tones from the other, making a two-mic approach the most effective (a). A single mic at a distance of several feet will also work (b).

The accordion is predominantly a mid-range instrument that doesn't require a mic with a greatly extended frequency response. Condenser and dynamic mics both work well for accordion. For distant miking, be sure the mic's response is relatively flat. Omnidirectional mics also work nicely for accordion; try using a closer placement than with directional mics for good stereo separation.

CHAPTER 16

Brass

Miking tips for the mighty brass.

The loud, bright tone of most brass instruments makes them a challenge to record well. If a mic picks up too much high-frequency content from trumpet, cornet or trombone, the resulting sound can be harsh and brittle. Capture too little high-frequency content, and the resulting brass sound may be dark and indistinct.

Though ribbon mics are popular for taking some of the edge off brass instruments, the more common condenser and dynamic mics can also give you great brass recordings. Mics with a predominant presence peak rarely work well for brass, as they tend to capture a somewhat piercing tone. A mic with a smooth, extended response in the highest register should be your first choice.

A directional mic's proximity effect can result in added warmth on the larger brass instruments, with little or no effect on trumpet or cornet. Omnidirectional mics work very well on brass instruments, sometimes capturing the most natural sound of the pickup pattern. The extremely high SPL of most brass instruments works in favor of the omni, making pickup of other instruments or unwanted room noises unlikely.

Try placing a mic 18 inches to several feet from the instrument. For a less natural sound, try emulating a live-sound approach by placing the mic extremely close to (or even inside) the bell. Some condenser mics designed to clip onto the bell of the instrument give excellent results for recording as well as live performance. If you have such a mic at your disposal, try it. A second mic several feet from the instrument may be a nice complement to the close-miked sound.

Brass instruments radiate high frequencies directly from their bells. Placing a mic directly on-axis with the instrument will give you the most crisp, defined sound. If this placement is strident or harsh, try placing the mic a few degrees above the bell, pointing down towards the player (Figure 16.1).

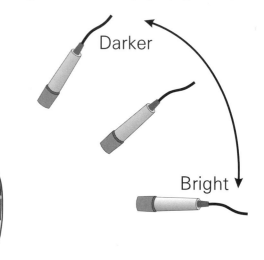

Figure 16.1. On-axis mic placement will give you a very bright sound from brass instruments. Swing the mic in an arc above the instrument to achieve a mellower sound.

Another option is to keep a directional mic directly in front of the bell, but rotate the mic itself for reduced treble pickup. For French horn (and to some degree, tuba), listeners are accustomed to hearing a predominantly off-axis sound. Try miking these instruments from a traditional listener vantage point instead of directly in front of the bell.

There's little or no advantage to miking a single brass instrument in a stereo configuration. When recording a brass ensemble, however, stereo recording techniques can be very effective. Spaced pair and coincident pair techniques can capture a cohesive ensemble sound with accurate stereo placement. If miking just two or three instruments, you may want to position a single mic in front of each one for more control over individual level, tone and stereo placement.

The last method for achieving nice stereo imaging from a brass ensemble is to double- or triple-track the brass parts. Simply position a small brass section around a single microphone and record several passes of the same parts. You can make minor changes to player position or musical arrangement to add some variety to each take. On mixdown, you can pan each take to a different stereo position for a large ensemble sound. This multi-track layering method works very well for most instruments.

CHAPTER 17

Woodwinds

From sax to piccolo, here's how to get great woodwind recordings.

Unlike brass instruments, woodwinds radiate most of their sound from the first few open holes rather than from the bell itself. A mic placement pointing down from slightly above the instrument lends itself to a good balance of tone from the holes, definition and air from the mouth area and sound from the bell.

A miking distance of 18 inches to several feet is a good place to start, though shorter distances may be appropriate when you need greater isolation. Close mic placement can exaggerate the mechanical sounds of keys and linkages on certain woodwinds, including the thunk of pads closing over holes. On flute and piccolo, too close a mic placement can make for a shrill, strident sound. On the plus side, few woodwinds put out fundamental tones low enough to be boosted greatly by proximity effect.

Mic a flute or piccolo from near the mouthpiece for a strong "chiff" or breath noise (see Figure 17.1 [a]). Try supplementing this close mic with a second mic in a more distant location. For a more natural flute sound with one mic, try placing the mic above and alongside the player's head, pointing down at the first finger hole (see Figure 17.1 [b]).

Miking a true reed woodwind (clarinet, oboe, bassoon) close to the mouthpiece rarely delivers a pleasing sound; a mic placement closer to the sound holes is usually preferred (see Figure 17.2). Condenser mics are the most common mics used for woodwinds, though some engineers rely on the smoothness of ribbon designs to mellow the sound of certain instruments. Few dynamic mics capture the full richness of tone from woodwind instruments, though the dynamic can work well for certain saxophone sounds. When miking a saxophone from extremely close to the bell, for example, the dynamic mic's less crisp sound can be a benefit.

Figure 17.2. Reed instruments sound most natural when miked from several feet away. The mouthpiece and bell regions will deliver a more colored—and potentially more appropriate—sound.

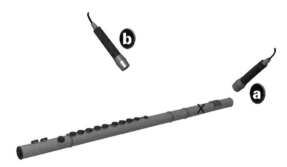

Figure 17.1. Miking flute and piccolo near the mouthpiece will result in a bright, breathy sound (a). For a more natural sound, try miking from above the instrument alongside the player's head (b).

Most saxophones record well with mic distances of several feet. Swinging the mic in an arc from in front of the bell to above the instrument changes the character of the sound considerably (see Figure 17.3). Experiment with placement until you achieve the desired balance of sound from the holes and bright overtones from the bell. A mic placed extremely close to the bell, as with a trumpet, may deliver the up-close sound suitable for many musical styles. Instead of placing the mic directly in-line with the bore of the sax, however, try placing the mic at a 45-degree angle a few inches from the bell for a more balanced sound. If this close-miking scheme gets you close to the sound you're after, try adding a more distant mic above the sax to round out the tone.

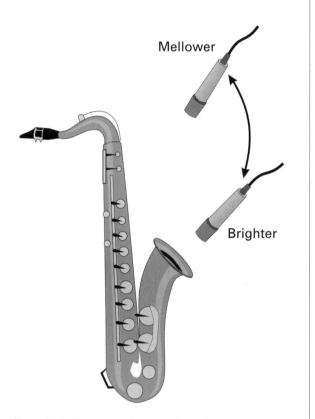

Mellower

Brighter

Figure 17.3. Where you mic a saxophone depends largely on the musical style and whether you want a bright, aggressive sound or a warmer, more natural tone.

Strings

Add some rosin to your recordings with great string sounds.

The smooth, velvety sound of a bowed string instrument has two main components: the string resonance of the instrument itself and the brush of the bow across the strings. A good string recording captures both of these in proper balance.

Condenser mics are best-suited for the rich harmonic texture of string instruments. Virtually any diaphragm size will work, but professionals usually gravitate toward large-diaphragm models when available. A dynamic mic will work in a pinch, though it may not capture the high-frequency air of the instrument.

Violin, viola and cello radiate their highest frequencies in a rather small arc perpendicular to the face of the instrument. Positioning the mic directly on-axis with the face gives the brightest, most articulate tone. For certain instruments (especially violins), this placement can sound strident and piercing. Moving the mic off-axis slightly will sometimes mellow and deepen the tone (see Figure 18.1).

Figure 18.1. String instruments radiate their brightest sound perpendicular to the instrument's face. Off-axis mic placement will give you a mellower tone.

Figure 18.2. A mic position a few inches from the bridge or f-hole captures a crisp, up-close sound from upright bass.

Traditionally, string instruments are miked from distances greater than two feet. Closer placement can create a somewhat choked and dark sound, especially when directional mics record the deeper-sounding viola or cello. Yet close-miking can be effective for certain modern styles of music. By adjusting the placement of a close mic, you can emphasize the string tone or the rosin sound of the bow.

When miking cello or double bass, a distant on-axis mic placement frequently brings with it phase cancellation from floor reflections. Try miking these solo instruments from a distance of 12 to 18 inches, directly off the bridge or f-hole area.

An upright bass is usually plucked instead of bowed. A shorter miking distance, such as just a few inches from the bridge or f-hole area, is appropriate (see Figure 18.2). A directional mic will give the bass added reinforcement due to proximity effect. Experiment with mic placement to get the best blend of fundamental tone and attack from the fingers.

When recording a string ensemble, all the guidelines for miking multiple instruments apply. Choose one or two mics with favorable response at distances of several feet; adjust player positions for best tonal balance (on- or off-axis) and level (distance from mic). Stereo miking techniques are very effective for string ensembles. If the room sound is agreeable, a room mic or two can add nice ambience to the recording. Classical engineers frequently place their main mics quite a distance from the players to capture a very smooth, cohesive sound.

CHAPTER 19

Vocals

Professional miking techniques for the most versatile of all instruments.

The human voice is the most complex and flexible instrument of all, capable of an incredibly broad range of expression, tone and volume. There's also a great deal of diversity from one voice to the next, which mandates a flexible, try-anything approach to vocal recording. Your first-choice vocal mic may sound wonderful on a strong baritone and horrid on a breathy soprano.

Most engineers' favorite vocal mics are large-diaphragm condensers that tend to capture a large, articulate vocal sound suitable for most types of music. But some small- and mid-sized diaphragms can achieve a similar vocal quality. And dynamic mics, though not usually a favorite for studio vocals, can deliver the perfect sound for some voices.

Because mic selection makes such a difference on vocals, it's not uncommon for engineers to record the same vocalist with different mics depending on the song and vocal delivery. The big, breathy sound of a large-diaphragm condenser may be perfect for a ballad, while the smaller, more focused sound of a vocal dynamic may better cut through a dense, up-tempo arrangement. When it comes time to choose a mic for a given vocalist or song, try every mic you've got; you may be surprised at which one sounds best.

While directional mics are most common for recording vocals, an omnidirectional mic can be very effective as well. An omni will exhibit no proximity effect, allowing you to place the mic much closer without bass buildup. An omni is also less prone to create popping noises, eliminating the need for a pop filter. The lack of proximity effect will also make for a more consistent sound if the vocalist changes distance from the mic. There will be a corresponding drop in level, but no significant change in tone. On mics with variable patterns, you can get good results from the intermediate patterns between cardioid and omni.

A good starting mic position for vocals is directly on-axis with the mouth, 6 to 12 inches away (see Figure 19.1 [a]). You may get a softer sound by placing the mic a few inches to either side of the mouth (figure 19.1 [b]). Placement above or below the mouth

can result in different vocal characters, which may be advantageous for certain voices. One popular off-axis mic placement is roughly 12 inches from the singer, at about forehead level, pointing down towards the mouth. Off-axis placement also has the advantage of reducing sibilance and popping.

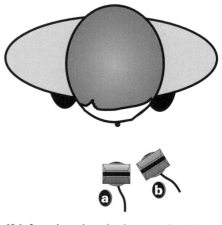

Figure 19.1. A good starting mic placement for solo vocals is 6 to 12 inches from the mouth (a). Off-axis placement can mellow a bright voice or help tame excessive sibilance (b).

Mic distance depends in large part on the room. A noisy or highly reverberant room (or one with poor-sounding acoustics) will require a closer mic placement, at which point proximity effect becomes a significant factor in the vocal sound. At six or eight inches away, certain directional mics generate enough bass boost to really muddy up a vocal sound. If your mic has a low-cut switch, it can clean up the bottom end of the vocal considerably.

Because most vocals are recorded at very close distances, even small shifts in mic or vocalist placement can make a dramatic difference in the sound. A shifty vocalist can make for punches or edits that are very obvious due to the change in level and/or vocal tone. When tracking vocals—especially with a directional mic—it's very important that mic distance and placement stay consistent throughout a session.

To this end, encourage the vocalist to make a mental note of his or her location. It may be helpful to have them frequently check the distance from their lips to the mic or pop filter with their fingers. As a last resort, place a line of tape on the floor where the vocalist can position his or her toes during recording. When miking from distances of a few feet or more, small changes in the vocalist's position are far less noticeable.

Sibilance is the bright burst of noise radiated by consonants such as "s," "t" and "f." With certain voices and mics, sibilance can be overpowering. One method for reducing sibilance with directional mics is to keep the mic directly in front of the mouth, while rotating it off-axis slightly. This reduces the high-frequency pickup of most mics and can eliminate problem sibilance. Ten or twenty degrees is usually enough to do the trick, depending on mic design and pickup pattern.

The most effective means of suppressing popping noises from plosives like "p" and "b" is the fabric pop filter. Stretched over a circular frame, the pop filter mounts to the mic stand or boom arm (see Figure 19.2). Foam filters, whether inside the mic or placed directly over it, are rarely as effective or as acoustically transparent. If you're using a vocal mic with a built-in pop filter, try removing the grill and foam filter and placing the mic behind a fabric pop filter instead. You can easily make your own pop filter with a pair of pantyhose and a 6- or 8-inch embroidery hoop.

Figure 19.2. An inexpensive pop filter can tame even the worst "p" and "b" sounds when recording vocals. (Courtesy AKG Acoustics)

For the vocalist who insists on holding the microphone during recording, here's a trick for pacifying them while still getting a clean vocal track. Set up your vocal mic of choice at a safe distance from the vocalist. Attach any handheld mic to a second cable and give it to the vocalist. The singer can then belt their most inspired performance into the placebo mic, while you capture the take without compromise with the more distant mic.

VOCAL ENSEMBLE

Recording a group of singers is much like recording any other ensemble. A large-diaphragm condenser is usually the mic of choice, though small- and mid-sized diaphragms can also deliver very good sound. Because ensemble recording almost always requires a somewhat distant mic placement, dynamic vocal mics (most having a presence peak) are rarely used for this application.

Mic placement and pickup pattern depend primarily on the size of the group and the characteristics of the recording space. You can get even pickup of two or three vocalists with a cardioid mic set about two feet from the group. More vocalists usually require placement of the cardioid mic at a greater distance where it will pick up more room ambience.

If recording four to six vocalists, try placing them in two groups on either side of a bidirectional mic. This will provide on-axis pickup of all the singers with minimal room ambience. Use distance and placement of individual singers to achieve a good blend of voices. Move louder voices back from the mic and place the brightest towards the edge of the mic's directional pattern. (For more information on miking groups, see Chapter 7.)

If you have a group of four vocalists who aren't afraid to get cozy, you can get excellent results by spacing them evenly around an omni mic. Since most omnis have some high-frequency attenuation at their sides (due to interference from the grill mount), turn the mic at a 45-degree angle relative to the vocalists (see Figure 19.3). There's no proximity effect from this miking setup. You can place the vocalists shoulder to shoulder around the mic for minimal room ambience.

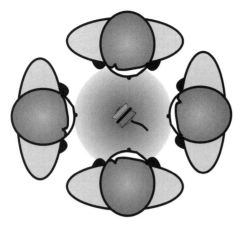

Figure 19.3. If recording a vocal group that's not afraid to get cozy, you can get excellent results putting them shoulder to shoulder around an omnidirectional mic.

Large ensembles require distant mic placement for even pickup, making the room's sound an unavoidable part of the recording. When an ensemble is large enough (a whole choir, for example), try traditional stereo miking techniques to record the group. Several mics spaced in front of the group will often deliver the most uniform sound. With a choir on risers, place the mics two or three feet from the front row, at roughly the same height as (and pointing at) the back row. If necessary, individual spot mics can be added for soloists.

4

Stereo Miking

In the early days of recording, musicians and vocalists gathered around a single microphone. Their performance was captured on a single track of tape and later played back through a single speaker. This was *monophonic* sound. Every instrument and voice appeared to be coming from the same point, as if an entire brass band was somehow packed inside grandma's AM radio console.

Today, we record and reproduce the vast majority of music in stereo: Two speakers or headphones create an expanse of sound where instruments and voices can come from any point between the speakers. Gone are the days when every sound fought for the same piece of sonic real estate.

With the arrival of stereo recording, microphone techniques evolved considerably. Engineers pioneered ways to capture the natural placement of instruments in an ensemble, lending greater distinction and more dramatic impact to their recordings. We call these "stereo miking" techniques, and they're the focus of this section.

CHAPTER 20

Stereo Miking Basics

Why two ears—and two mics—are better than one.

Stereo miking refers to any miking arrangement where we position and aim microphones (usually two) to capture the left-to-right imaging of one or more sound sources. Traditionally, the term has meant something more than just using multiple mics and panning their signals through the stereo soundfield. Close-miking three rack toms and panning them left to right constitutes stereo recording, not stereo miking.

Several stereo miking techniques have become popular over the years. Though some audio purists speak of stereo miking as if it were an arcane, black art, the principles are simple and effective enough to be used by any home studio owner. Rest assured, stereo miking is *not* just for classical music.

LOCALIZATION 101

Our auditory system uses many cues to discern the location of a sound. Over the years, scientists have found ways to quantify, capture and even fabricate these cues. As sound recordists, we're most interested in the two simple cues related to lateral position: amplitude and delay (or phase).

Amplitude cues are probably the simplest of all: If a sound is louder in one ear than the other, our brain assumes the sound is closer to that ear. This is the principle behind the pan controls on an audio mixer and the balance control on a stereo receiver. Making a sound louder in one speaker shifts the perceived location of that sound toward the louder speaker; when the level difference between speakers reaches roughly 20dB, we perceive the sound to be coming from just one speaker (see Figure 20.1 [a]).

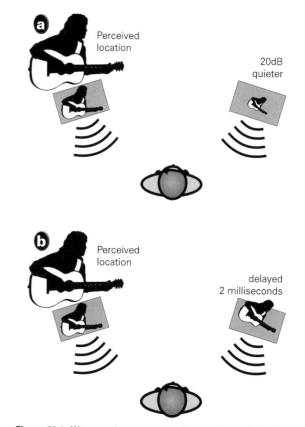

Figure 20.1. We perceive a sound to be coming entirely from one speaker when the opposite speaker is at least 20dB quieter (a) or delayed by roughly 2 milliseconds (b).

Delay cues result from the distance between our ears. If a sound source sits on either side of a listener, sound will arrive at the nearest ear slightly earlier than the other. The brain perceives the sound as being closer to whichever ear heard it first. With high-frequency sounds, the brain recognizes the extremely short delay between the two ears; the brain uses a different kind of cue (phase shift) to localize low-frequency sounds. In a stereo speaker system, slightly delaying the signal arriving at one speaker (without changing its volume) shifts the perceived source location toward the non-delayed speaker. A delay of just under 2ms will make a sound appear to come entirely from the undelayed speaker (see Figure 20.1 [b]).

Alone, either of these cues allows the brain to localize a sound. Together, these cues make for a more pronounced effect. This is how we hear in the real world; the ear picks up both amplitude and arrival time differences (delay). Stereo miking techniques that capture both cues generate the most dramatic imaging.

GOALS IN STEREO

There are at least seven goals of traditional stereo miking. The more of these a given stereo recording method accomplishes, the more effective and natural the resulting sound. Good stereo miking should:

1. Accurately capture the lateral positions of instruments or voices. If an instrument is 35 degrees to the left of center in an ensemble, its playback should seem to come from that same angle between the speakers. A stereo spread that's unnaturally narrow will place the sound too close to the center. An exaggerated spread will be too wide, placing the sound too close to the left speaker.

2. Capture sound that spreads all the way between the speakers. Sounds at the outer edges of an ensemble should appear to come completely from one speaker or the other. If a stereo recording is too narrow, the outermost sounds will appear to come from a position just inside the speakers.

3. Allow the listener to clearly distinguish the positions of various instruments. If the stereo imaging is not sharp, instruments and voices will appear to blur into one another.

4. Preserve the tonal balance of the sounds regardless of position. Frequency response should be even across the full stereo soundfield.

5. Capture an appropriate amount of room ambience.

6. Ensure that the relative level of instruments is even across the stereo image, with no dips or hot spots. A miking arrangement that emphasizes instruments on the outer edges of the ensembles will appear to leave a hole in the middle of the soundfield.

7. Capture a sound whose frequency response stays consistent when summed in mono.

Note that all of these goals don't apply for every application. In pop music, for example, an exaggerated stereo spread may be just the effect you're after. Unfortunately, some stereo effects and miking techniques can create cancellation of certain frequencies when stereo signals are played on mono systems. This phenomenon, known as mono compatibility, may not be a great concern, especially if you're not making music destined for television or AM radio broadcast. A stereo miking setup that captures little or no ambience may be appropriate in rooms with less-than-perfect reverb qualities. As with all aspects of miking, you should tailor your approach to capture the specific sound you're after.

Because it's a somewhat specialized application, certain mics work better than others for stereo miking. Mics with very flat frequency responses and high sensitivities generally offer the best performance, which is why engineers use condenser mics almost exclusively in stereo miking. The even off-axis response of small-diaphragm condenser mics makes them a popular choice.

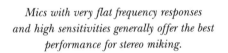

Mics with very flat frequency responses and high sensitivities generally offer the best performance for stereo miking.

Dynamic mics usually lack the sensitivity and flat response required for an uncolored recording. Directional mics with a built-in presence boost can sound too thin for stereo miking. Like any facet of recording, however, these are guidelines and not absolutes. You may get the perfect coloration from a pair of inexpensive dynamic vocal mics in a stereo arrangement.

CHAPTER 21

Stereo Miking Setups

Four easy recipes for lush stereo sound.

There are four common miking arrangements for stereo recording: coincident pair (or X-Y), near-coincident pair, spaced pair and mid-side (or M/S). Each has advantages and disadvantages, and some are more suitable for certain types of music or instruments than others. Engineers also use a few more esoteric methods for some applications, though rarely in home studios.

COINCIDENT PAIR OR X-Y

Coincident pair miking uses two directional mics angled between 90 and 135 degrees apart, their capsules placed as close together as possible, usually with one mic above the other (see Figure 21.1). Sounds to the left or right of center hit one mic on-axis and one off-axis; this causes a difference in level between the two mics. Because the mics are *coincident*, sound from all directions arrives at both capsules at the same time; this setup doesn't generate time difference cues.

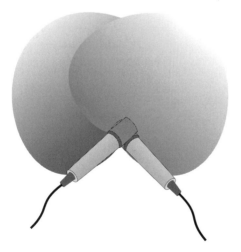

Figure 21.1. Coincident pair stereo miking places two mics at an angle, with their elements as close together as possible. Coincident pairs generate amplitude cues, but no delay cues.

This type of stereo miking offers very distinct localization for instruments through the soundstage, with positions sharply defined. Stereo spread is accurate, though usually a bit on the narrow side. One big plus with coincident pair miking is its mono compatibility. Since there's no appreciable time difference between the left and right signals, combining them in mono doesn't cause phase cancellation problems.

You can use cardioid, supercardioid or hyper-cardioid patterns in coincident pair miking. The tighter the pattern and greater the angle between mics, the broader the stereo image. Angling hyper-cardioid mics at roughly 100 degrees, for example, delivers a good sense of spaciousness and depth. Angle the mics out too far, however, and the middle of the stereo image can start to sound hollow and indistinct. This happens because sounds coming from the middle hit both mics off-axis, where most cardioid and cardioid-derivative patterns have a reduced high-frequency response.

One variation on the coincident pair arrangement is called the Blumlein or Stereosonic technique. It uses two bidirectional mics in place of directional mics and angles them at 90 degrees (see Figure 21.2). Definition of the stereo image is excellent and wide, and the placement and width of reverb and room ambience are very natural. The main drawback of this technique is that sounds that lie more than 45 degrees from center hit the front lobe of one mic and the back lobe of the other with nearly equal intensity. Because the two mic signals are out of phase, this compromises the stereo imaging for these sounds.

Figure 21.2. One variation on the stereo coincident pair places two bidirectional mics at 90 degrees. This miking technique is called a Blumlein pair.

Since you don't want sounds to fall outside the Blumlein's 90-degree spread, the width of the ensemble dictates how far away the mics sit. This makes it impossible to control the amount of ambience recorded by changing mic distance. The Blumlein's 90-degree limit often makes a more distant (and reverberant) mic position than an engineer would otherwise use. The Blumlein technique generally picks up strong room ambience anyway, making this mic arrangement of little use in live recording spaces or those with poor reverb character.

NEAR-COINCIDENT PAIR

The near-coincident pair setup is similar to coincident pair. The primary difference is the introduction of some distance between the mic capsules. This gap between the mics creates time difference information as well as level information. The result is a sharply defined stereo image with a greater sense of depth and realism than from a coincident pair. Stereo width is good, though not quite as dramatic as Blumlein or spaced omni arrangements. Because of the time delay between mics, near-coincident pair recordings don't fare well when summed in mono.

There are many established starting points for near-coincident mic placement. The ORTF technique (established by the French Broadcasting Organization) specifies angling cardioid mics at 110 degrees, with a capsule-to-capsule spacing of roughly seven inches. The Dutch Broadcasting Foundation's NOS system suggests spacing cardioid mics at 12 inches apart, at an angle of 90 degrees. Another common technique places cardioid mics at the same 90 degree angle, but with just 8 inches between capsules. Each

of these methods has its own unique characteristics in the areas of stereo spread, realism, imaging sharpness, depth and ambient pickup; experimentation is the key to finding the right setup for your needs (see Figure 21.3).

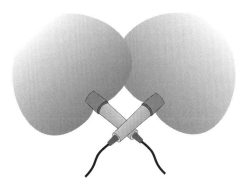

Figure 21.3. A near-coincident pair angles two directional mics apart, but spaces their capsules apart by several inches. This miking scheme captures amplitude and delay cues.

None of the standard near-coincident arrangements specify mics with a tighter pattern than cardioid. Though you may have luck with near-coincident supercardioids or hypercardioids, the result is likely to exhibit an exaggerated stereo spread with a hollow-sounding middle image. Spacing out bidirectional mics (a modified Blumlein technique, for example) would create similar problems and is not commonly done.

SPACED PAIR

The third stereo miking technique points two mics in the same direction (directly forward) with a large space between them (see Figure 21.4). Sounds from directly in the middle arrive at both mics at the same time. Sounds to either side arrive at one mic slightly sooner than the other. This generates time delay cues but no significant amplitude differences. In that sense, the spaced pair technique is just the opposite of the coincident pair (which generates amplitude cues but no time difference). Any pickup pattern works well in the spaced pair arrangement, though omnidirectional mics are most common.

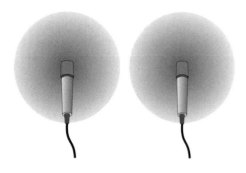

Figure 21.4. Spaced pair stereo miking places two directional or omnidirectional mics three or more feet apart. Spaced pairs generate delay cues but no significant amplitude cues.

A distance of just two feet between mics will generate enough delay to position the outermost sounds completely in one speaker or the other on playback. Unfortunately, positioning two closely spaced mics in front of an ensemble causes stronger pickup of those voices or instruments in the middle. Greater distances between mics (up to as much as 10 or 12 feet) are common, as the larger spacing picks up a better balance of sound between the edges and center of the group.

A larger spacing between mics produces much longer delay times, making sounds even slightly off-center seem to come completely from one speaker. This creates an unnatural "hole in the middle" sound, where most instruments or voices seem to be coming from the outermost edges of the soundstage. One solution is to add a third mic in between the main two mics. Panned to the center and mixed with the other two, this mic helps restore a more natural stereo image (see Figure 21.5).

Sound Source

Figure 21.5. When an ensemble requires a very wide spaced pair, center imaging suffers. A third middle mic helps restore the center image.

Spaced pair miking generally delivers a smooth, spacious sound. Stereo placement is somewhat vague for instruments located off-center, with sounds tending to blur into one another. For certain types of music, the blending effect of stereo pair miking is appropriate. Reverberation is broad and lush with the stereo pair, wrapping around the listener in a dra-

matic (though not entirely natural) fashion.

Most engineers prefer to use omnis in spaced pair miking due to their full, extended bass response. Omnidirectional mics also pick up the greatest degree of ambience from reverberant rooms, making the characteristics of the room a critical factor in the quality of the recording. Mics with cardioid or tighter patterns will pick up considerably less reverb when used in a spaced pair arrangement, and you can position them further from the ensemble to ensure even coverage.

Because spaced pair miking generates significant time delays, combining the left and right signals in mono can create noticeable phase cancellation. The frequency and severity of the cancellation depends on numerous variables, but in some cases they are strong enough to cause problems for mono playback. For most stereo music recording, the spaced pair technique works very well.

MID-SIDE OR M/S

Mid-side stereo miking is a specialized type of coincident pair miking, using one cardioid (or tighter) mic and one bidirectional mic. This technique points the bidirectional mic perpendicular to the soundfield and the directional mic directly towards it (see Figure 21.6). By changing the relative level of the two mics' output, you can remotely control the pickup pattern and stereo spread of the recording. Adding a small amount of the bidirectional mic's output to the forward-pointing mic creates a narrow stereo image. Increasing the bidirectional mic's output creates a much wider stereo image.

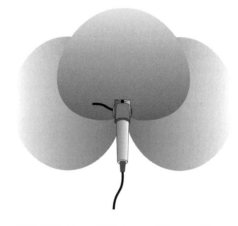

Figure 21.6. Mid-side or M/S stereo miking combines a front-facing directional mic with a side-facing bidirectional mic. Mid-side miking captures amplitude cues but no delay cues.

To hear the M/S-recorded signal in a normal listening environment, M/S miking uses a special decoding arrangement, which you can create yourself or purchase in a dedicated mid-side processor. With either approach, the bidirectional mic's output is split and one side is phase-reversed. You then pan these outputs hard left and hard right (usually with the inverted signal panned right), adding the directional mic's output to the mix in the center (see Figure 21.7). The left signal then consists of the mid mic's output plus the side mic, the right signal consists of the mid mic minus the side mic.

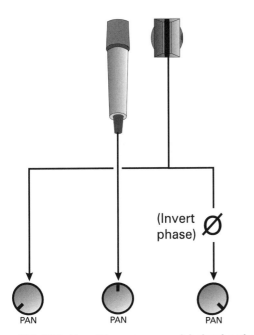

Figure 21.7. Mid-side miking uses a special signal path to decode the M/S signals into standard left and right signals. Decoding can be done before or after recording.

We call this conversion of the two mics' signals into a stereo signal the M/S decode process. Note that you can perform the decode process at two different stages: before recording or upon playback. The former results in a standard left and right signal being recorded, at which point you can no longer change the spaciousness and width of the stereo image. Decoding on playback means that you record the output of the two mics separately, which allows you to adjust the stereo image as you mix.

Localization accuracy of the mid-side method is very good. Sounds in the center of the soundstage are picked up predominantly by the mid microphone, which gives M/S recordings a very sharp middle image. Mono compatibility of mid-side miking is excellent. Combining the left and right signals in mono cancels the output of the bidirectional mic, leaving the output of the front-facing mid mic only.

This eliminates potential phase shift or off-axis coloration from multiple mics. The mid mic also picks up less reverberation than the side mic, which results in a cleaner mono signal.

There are several other stereo miking techniques and systems in use in music recording, though they're used far less frequently than the ones already mentioned. Binaural stereo recording places two small microphones on either side of a human or dummy head (see Figure 21.8). These mics pick up sound colored by the high-frequency shadowing of the human head, which is another localization cue our brains use to discern sound direction. Binaural techniques create recordings with uncanny realism when played back through headphones. Unfortunately, the effect is less dramatic when played back through regular stereo loudspeakers.

Figure 21.8. Binaural stereo recording uses a dummy head and microphone ears to create uncanny stereo imaging when played back through headphones. (Courtesy Neumann USA)

Other stereo miking techniques use two microphones separated by an acoustic baffle. Some use omnidirectional condensers spaced a few inches from a padded disk, others splay pressure-zone mics at an angle on either side of a foam barrier (see Figure 21.9). One extremely expensive system arranges four large-diaphragm condenser elements in the shape of a tetrahedron, offering remote control over a nearly infinite number of directional patterns.

Figure 21.9. The Crown SASS-P MkII stereo mic places two boundary mics on either side of a foam baffle. (Courtesy Crown International)

Though these techniques and products may be of less use to the home studio recordist, they illustrate an important point: There's no "right" way to capture stereo sound, and an unorthodox approach may deliver just what you're looking for. For example, some engineers record drum kits by attaching small condenser mics to the sides of the drummer's head in a semi-binaural arrangement. This "drummer's ear view" of the instrument makes for a fresh, unique sound unobtainable with traditional stereo miking techniques.

CHAPTER 22

Stereo Miking: Why and When

How to know when stereo miking is the right approach for a recording.

Sometimes, we use stereo miking when the size of an ensemble makes close-miking impractical. In these situations, one of the four miking techniques listed in the previous chapter will usually deliver good sound and a pleasing stereo image. Even when a group is small enough to devote a mic to each musician or vocalist, you may want to use a stereo miking arrangement instead.

Close-miking individuals and panning them electronically will create a definite stereo image, but remember that pan knobs generate amplitude differences only. Stereo placement methods that create both time and amplitude differences often make for the most dramatic stereo imaging. The more distant stereo miking scheme will also pick up considerably more room ambience and reverberation, which can add a sense of space and air around the musicians.

Even when a group is small enough to devote a mic to each musician or vocalist, you may want to use a stereo miking arrangement instead.

Stereo miking can be very effective when recording a single musician or vocalist. Instead of using a pan control to position a single mic signal in the mix, set up stereo mics and place the sound source off-center (see Figure 22.1). The resulting stereo image will be much more natural than that achieved by pan controls alone. Try recording a percussionist with a spaced pair of mics, allowing the musician to place each instrument in the mix by changing its position in front of the mics. If you've got the available tracks, experiment with recording a whole song using stereo mic techniques exclusively for sound placement. The resulting sound may impress you with its natural, open stereo imaging.

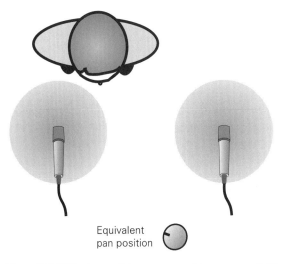

Equivalent
pan position

Figure 22.1. With stereo miking, you can achieve very realistic stereo imaging of voices or instruments without using a mixer's pan controls.

Stereo miking can also capture a wide, spacious sound from a single instrument. Piano, acoustic guitar and vibes are examples of instruments that sound great when captured with a stereo miking technique (such as spaced pair). Placing the mics close to the instrument will pick up a dry sound with a dramatic stereo spread; distant placement will pick up more room sound and less dramatic stereo.

Some instruments and recording spaces lend themselves to a dual-miking approach, with one pair of mics up close and a second pair placed at a distance. The more distant mics will add a nice ambience to the close-miked sound without compromising the stereo image. These two pairs of mics needn't use the same technique. You could supplement an up-close spaced pair with a more distant mid-side setup (see Figure 22.2).

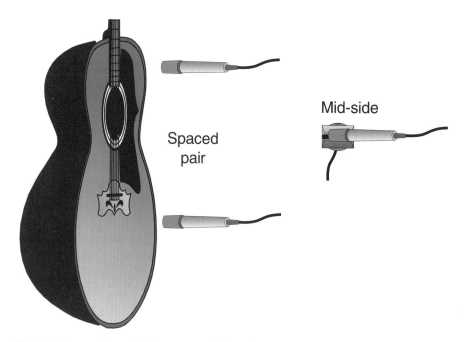

Spaced pair

Mid-side

22.2. Combining up-close and distant stereo miking schemes can result in a full, spacious sound.

CHAPTER 23

Stereo Microphones and Matched Pairs

Great stereo sound, right out of the box.

There are many stereo microphones available today that include two mic elements in the same housing (see Figure 23.1). These mics commonly use either a coincident pair (X-Y) or mid-side (M/S) approach; a few offer both. Stereo mics are convenient and generally deliver very good sound, but they don't offer as much flexibility as two discrete mics. You can't do spaced pair miking, for example, with an all-in-one mic.

Stereo mics are convenient and generally deliver very good sound, but they don't offer as much flexibility as two discrete mics.

Most stereo mics offer a pattern control, located either on the mic itself or on an external box. In a coincident pair stereo mic, this control adjusts the angle between the two mic elements. In a mid-side design, the pattern control changes the relative blend of the mid (forward facing) and side mics. Those mics that offer both X-Y and M/S do so by way of elements with selectable patterns. In X-Y mode, both elements are usually cardioid (or tighter); in M/S mode, at least one element switches to a bi-directional pattern. Some mics also offer low-cut filters, attenuators and other controls. Virtually all stereo mics use condenser elements and draw power from either a phantom supply or built-in battery.

Engineers use stereo mics primarily in field recording for ENG (electronic news gathering), movie soundtracks, special audio effects, television and some classical music recordings. Few home studio owners use stereo mics, primarily because of their high cost. If you can find a good deal on a stereo mic, however, you'll likely be happy with the resulting sound.

THE MATCHED PAIR

Many manufacturers sell pairs of mics specifically for stereo recording (see Figure 23.2). In most cases, the manufacturer simply bundles two mics of the same model in a single case for sale as a stereo kit. With the high degree of consistency and quality control achieved by most manufacturers, the result is a stereo pair that's similar enough in sound for most stereo miking applications. In fewer cases, the manufacturer actually tests and pairs up mics having nearly identical frequency response and sensitivity performance.

Figure 23.1. Audio-Technica AT825 X-Y stereo mic. (Courtesy Audio-Technica)

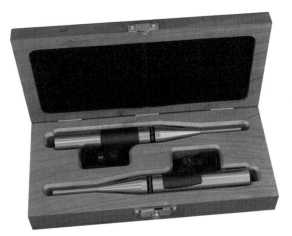

Figure 23.2. When you buy a matched pair of mics, they'll offer nearly identical performance for the best possible stereo imaging. (Courtesy Earthworks)

Using a matched pair for stereo miking helps ensure an even, natural image across the stereo soundfield. Any sonic differences in a stereo pair compromises the stereo image, which is why professionals use a matched pair almost exclusively for stereo miking. The only exception to this is the M/S miking method, which uses both a bidirectional and directional mic. Matching the sonic quality of the two mics is not as important with M/S stereo, which is a good thing. It's nearly impossible to get identical performances out of two mics with different polar patterns.

Shopping for Microphones

Buying microphones can be a tricky proposition. Folks in the market for a microphone quickly discover a bewildering number of models to choose from. To make matters worse, objective information can be almost impossible to come by.

Sound familiar? If this describes your latest mic buying experience, this is the section for you. Whether your mic budget is $100 or $5,000, the following tips will give you lots of practical advice for finding, testing and buying microphones and will help you find the perfect mic for your needs.

CHAPTER 24

Navigating the Microphine Buying Maze

How to avoid getting lost on your quest for the perfect mic.

Sometimes, it seems there's a conspiracy to make buying mics as difficult as possible. Manufacturers often grant their mics near-magical properties in ads and literature, making it difficult to tell the truth from the hype. Music stores, if they carry microphones, rarely have an environment conducive to the kind of objective audition you need. Finally, all the expert advice in the world won't guarantee you end up with the right mic for *your* needs in *your* studio. No two people hear things exactly the same, and one person's perfect sound is another's worst sonic nightmare.

That said, here are several tried-and-true principles to help you shop the microphone market.

THE PRICE IS RIGHT

The old axiom "price isn't everything" really applies to microphone purchases. *Sound* is everything, and the sonic quality of a microphone doesn't always parallel its price tag. Professional engineers use inexpensive mics on big-budget albums every day. An inexpensive dynamic mic may see as much use in a professional studio as a $5,000 tube condenser model. When a mic is right for a particular instrument or voice, it's right regardless of its manufacturing pedigree or list price.

In the microphone market, models bearing certain names command a higher price than comparable models from other manufacturers. Whether the resulting sonic difference justifies the added expense depends on whom you ask. In some cases, these high-dollar mics are popular in studios where the client "wow factor" is an important element in attracting and keeping business. In reality, mics costing one-half to one-third as much can offer similar performance, especially to the untrained ear of the average listener. The bottom line is this: You *can* capture great-sounding recordings with affordable mics. Manufacturers that tell you differently are usually trying to sell you a more expensive model.

In all fairness, there usually are quantifiable differences between a $5,000 mic and one closer to $1,000. You'll rarely spot these differences in the specifications; they'll be most noticeable in the character and personality of the mic. If you can't afford a $5,000 mic, there are other ways to endow your recordings with character and personality.

Though price isn't everything, there is a class of ultra-affordable (read "cheap") mics you'll do well to avoid. These are often high-impedance designs with a permanently attached ¼-inch or ⅛-inch jack cable. Designed for karaoke singing or dictation into a portable recorder, these mics often have limited and very uneven frequency responses, unpredictable off-axis performance and low sensitivities. Staying in the realm of professional mics (XLR connectors, recognizable names and list prices above about $150) will ensure good sound.

SHOP THE USED MIC MARKET

Most microphones are very sturdy devices, providing decades of reliable service if not abused. Few studios live this long, making it easy to find used mics for sale. If a used microphone has been cared for, it may be an excellent purchase for the budget-minded home studio owner.

You can capture great-sounding recordings with affordable mics.

Apart from studios closing and liquidating their equipment, there are several other avenues to explore for used mics. Live sound companies often sell off equipment periodically, even if they're not going out of business, and may have numerous dynamic and small-diaphragm condenser mics for sale. Music stores and rental companies sell off their rental stock periodically. They often sell mics based on how *long* they've been in circulation, not how many times they've been rented. It's possible to find several-year-old rental mics that are in like-new condition.

Classified ads sometimes pay off for the used mic hunter, especially when an individual or studio runs a "selling everything" ad. These often indicate a frustrated musician getting out of music or a troubled company liquidating gear. Both can lead to excellent used mic deals. Though it's a rare occurrence, some people have found incredible used mic deals at yard sales. If the folks having the yard sale are not knowledgeable about the mics, they will be happy to sell them for a fraction of what they're worth. We've probably all heard stories of a lucky buyer picking up a matched pair of vintage large-diaphragm condenser mics for less than $100 at a yard sale.

MICROPHONE GERIATRICS

When it comes to buying used microphones, there are two principles to keep in mind: 1) old isn't always bad, and 2) vintage isn't always good. Just like today, past decades have seen their share of brilliant mic designs and absolute clunkers in the mic market. An old mic found at a pawn shop or flea market could be a nearly useless relic or an incredible bargain (see Figure 24.1). If you are shopping dusty shelves and back rooms for a vintage mic, keep your eyes open for names like Neumann, Telefunken, AKG, RCA and Western Electric. If in decent condition, these mics can represent a very good investment.

At the same time, don't automatically assume other old mics are of no value. Even mics with no collector appeal whatsoever can be useful in certain recording situations. Studio lore is full of stories where a cheap, no-name, 50-year-old mic delivered the perfect sound for a specific instrument or voice. Low-fidelity recordings are back in style for many genres of music, and old mics can be a great way to capture a compact, gritty sound.

If a used microphone has been cared for, it may be an excellent purchase for the budget-minded home studio owner.

Aged mics that don't work at all can still be a good investment, but they may require a considerable amount of money to be brought to working condition. If a 40-year-old condenser mic needs a new capsule, you could be looking at a $2,000-3,000 repair. The repaired mic may be worth twice that amount, but the initial investment might be prohibitive for many.

If you have no desire to resuscitate a damaged mic, and you can't test the mic out on the spot, you're taking a gamble in purchasing an old microphone. There's no sure-fire way to tell if a mic is still func-

tional by looking at it, and a bruised and dented case doesn't always mean the mic is damaged.

Figure 24.1. If you run across a vintage mic like the Neumann CMV-3 "bottle" at a yard sale, snatch it up. The CMV-3, introduced in 1930 as the first condenser mic, fetches upward of $5,000 on the vintage mic market. (Courtesy Neumann USA)

CHAPTER 25

Try Before You Buy

Use your ears before you pull out your wallet.

You'd never dream of buying a car without driving it first or an expensive jacket without trying it on. Yet a surprising number of people are willing to purchase a microphone without hearing it first. Maybe they simply don't think there is that much difference from model to model or maybe they're forced to purchase mics from a source where hands-on tests are impossible. Either way, the end result is a hit-or-miss purchase that may not get you the mic you're looking for.

If possible, try and find a way to test the mic in your own studio before purchasing. A local music store may allow you to try the mic at home with a refundable deposit or you may know someone who could lend you the mic you plan to purchase. In some cases, the store will give you a few days to return a mic purchase if it doesn't meet your needs. Don't be afraid to take advantage of such a policy to find the right microphone. Mail order companies may offer a similar return policy, only charging you the cost of return shipping a mic that didn't suit your purposes.

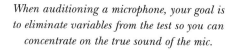

If possible, try and find a way to test the mic in your own studio before purchasing.

If your city has even a modest recording scene, you may find companies that rent all sorts of recording equipment, including microphones. A one-day rental of a mic (or two) won't set you back much money and may save you from making a bad purchase. Rent several mics and try them on different instruments and voices. You'll learn more about mics' performance when comparing them to one another and to mics you're very familiar with.

Remember that rental mics are used and may have experienced all sorts of abuse or misuse. In spite of a rental company's best efforts to keep them in top shape, a rental mic may not sound like it should. If you question the performance of a rental mic, you may be able to swap it for another unit. At the very least, you shouldn't have to pay for that mic's rental.

When auditioning mics, remember that there will be differences in sound even between two new mics of the same make and model. Certain manufacturers turn out mics with very consistent quality, while others don't have such elaborate facilities for quality control. Some low-cost, large-diaphragm condenser mics use capsules imported from China; these have a reputation for somewhat inconsistent performance. If you can try out several mics from the same batch, you'll be able to hand-pick the one that sounds best to your ears.

THE TEST DRIVE

If you have the opportunity to test out microphones at a music store or similar location, there are some things you can do to stack the odds in favor of an uncolored, objective test. These simple techniques may seem odd to some people (the salesperson, for example), but they're the best way to ensure a wise mic purchase in a less-than-optimum testing environment. All these techniques have the same basic goal: Eliminate variables from the test so you can concentrate on the true sound of the mic(s).

Bring a friend along who plays an instrument or sings, depending on the mic's main application. Playing or singing yourself makes it impossible to really hear what the mic is picking up. In the case of using your own voice, the bones of the skull carry enough sound to color any non-recorded test. The optimum subject for your mic test is someone you've recorded in the past, someone whose sound you're familiar with.

When auditioning a microphone, your goal is to eliminate variables from the test so you can concentrate on the true sound of the mic.

Bring your most-trusted pair of headphones along and use them instead of the store's PA speakers or monitors. Much better than listening to strange speakers in an unfamiliar room, headphones give you a familiar point of reference. They will also make your assistant less self-conscious as they sing or play into the mic(s) and will eliminate the possibility of feedback. Finally, headphones (sealed headphones are preferable) will tend to block out the competing sounds in the store. Most mixers have headphone amps built in, the fidelity of which is usually more than adequate for this purpose.

Eliminate all processing from the signal path, including outboard equalizers, dynamics controllers or effects processors. If the mixer has an EQ bypass switch, engage it; if not, set all gain pots to their center detent position. The best-case scenario is a mixer with pre-fader solo, which will give you the cleanest signal path for the microphone. If you're testing more than one mic, be sure to match their levels precisely with the mixer's input trim control. We tend to favor louder sounds, making it nearly impossible to compare two mics with mismatched levels.

When testing more than one mic, have your singer/musician sing or play the same distance from both mics. Ideally, you should set up both mics side by side so you can switch between them with the mixer's solo buttons. You may want to experiment with mic placement and distance as well. After a few minutes of comparing the mics, you should have a very clear picture of their sonic differences.

If the store has a studio-like environment for testing mics and other recording products, your job is easier. It's still important to watch mic placement carefully and be certain there's no EQ or other processing in the signal chain. If the studio has multiple monitors, select those most similar to your own monitors. If the studio doesn't have familiar monitors, or if you aren't comfortable with the sound of the room, monitor the mic test with your headphones.

CHAPTER 26

Your Microphone Budget

How to get the most from your mic dollar.

Deciding how many mics you need is an important step in the mic buying process. Having dozens of high-quality mics at your disposal is clearly the best setup, as this increases your odds of finding a mic well suited to every instrument and voice you record. In reality, few people have that kind of money to invest in their microphones.

Even with a moderate microphone budget ($500, for example), there are at least two approaches to purchasing microphones. One involves spending the money on several decent-quality microphones, say six dynamic mics costing roughly $75 each. If you need to mic multiple instruments or voices at one time, this may be the best approach.

For most studios, however, buying one or two good-quality condenser mics is a better use of the mic budget. Such mics will usually capture much more accurate sound than inexpensive dynamic models. Condenser mics will be more versatile, delivering better recordings from a broad range of instruments. Relatively few home studios record drums or groups where numerous mics are needed; most home recordings are built up track by track by one or two musicians.

For most studios, buying one or two good-quality condenser mics is the best use of the mic budget.

Buying two similar model condensers gives you the option of using stereo miking techniques, as well as recording two different instruments or voices at the same time. Buying a single condenser microphone allows you to acquire an even higher-quality mic, possibly a large-diaphragm model. Most large-diaphragm condensers will do a great job on the majority of instruments and are preferred for vocal recording. Certain large-diaphragm condensers have grown quite affordable (some under $500) and may represent the best investment for the home studio owner.

How many mics to purchase and what type they should be is a decision you can make only after a thoughtful analysis of your recording style and needs. Since it's not feasible for most people to own enough mics to cover every possible recording situation, occasionally renting or borrowing mics is a good option. If you know other home studio owners in your area, you may want to invest in a common mic pool for everyone to use.

Though every studio's mic requirements are different, here are some guidelines for purchasing the most versatile combination of microphones. These are not absolutes; use these recommendations as starting points as you make your own mic purchases. Note that the following list is largely price independent, meaning it's possible to spend anywhere from several hundred to several thousand dollars for any combination of mics.

If you're buying:	Consider:
one mic	large-diaphragm condenser, or small-diaphragm condenser
two mics	pair small-diaphragm condensers, or large-diaphragm condenser and instrument dynamic
three mics	large-diaphragm condenser, small-diaphragm condenser and instrument dynamic, or large-diaphragm condenser and pair small-diaphragm condensers
four mics	large-diaphragm condenser, pair small-diaphragm condensers and instrument dynamic
five or more mics	large-diaphragm condenser, pair small-diaphragm condensers and pair instrument dynamics

6

Microphone Buyer's Guide

Now that we've covered mic theory and technique, it's time to check out the tools of our trade. What follows are photos, specs and frequency/polar charts (where available) for 70 mics from over 20 manufacturers. Though many of these mics do double-duty for studio and stage use, most are designed specifically for recording. This list represents a small sampling of the mics available to the home studio recordist and is not meant to be comprehensive.

For those multi-pattern mics that have frequency response and polar charts available, I've included them for the cardioid pattern only. Where specs differ between the patterns, I've listed those for the cardioid pattern as well. This makes it easier to compare the performance of these mics to other single-pattern models.

Icons show some of the instruments and miking applications appropriate for that model. These applications are also not meant to be comprehensive; a given mic may be well-suited for an instrument whose icon does not appear. Trying a mic on a specific instrument is the only way to be sure it's a good fit.

Those models marked with the "Author's Pick" logo I have found to provide great sound quality, versatility and, most importantly, good value for the money. Your mileage will vary, of course, so take these recommendations with the usual grain of salt. Remember, *you* decide what sounds good and what doesn't.

The mics are broken into three list price categories: under $500 (Chapter 27), $500-1,000 (Chapter 28) and $1,000-1,500 (Chapter 29). These categories reflect list prices as of August, 1997. Microphone prices may have changed by the time you read this, which is why individual prices for each mic are not listed.

Please use Appendix B: Microphone Manufacturers as a resource to learn more about these mics. Where appropriate, we've listed World Wide Web addresses. Manufacturer web pages are a great way to gather information about microphones.

CHAPTER 27

Microphones Under $500

| Acoustic Guitar | Bass Instruments | Brass | Cymbals | Drums | Electric Guitar | Percussion | Piano | Strings | Vocals | Woodwinds |

MAKE AND MODEL: **AKG C1000S**

TYPE: **condenser**

PICKUP PATTERN: **cardioid, hypercardioid (w/PPC 1000)**

FREQUENCY RESPONSE: **50Hz-20kHz**

SENSITIVITY: **6mV/Pa**

NOISE: **19dBA**

MAXIMUM SPL: **137dB at 0.5% THD**

IMPEDANCE: **200 ohms**

FEATURES: **internal battery or phantom power operation**

MAKE AND MODEL: **AKG C418**

TYPE: **condenser**

PICKUP PATTERN: **hypercardioid**

FREQUENCY RESPONSE: **50Hz-20kHz**

SENSITIVITY: **4mV/Pa (-48dBV)**

MAXIMUM SPL: **131dB at 1% THD**

IMPEDANCE: **< 200 ohms**

ALSO AVAILABLE FROM AKG:

C416, C419 condenser instrument mics

MAKE AND MODEL: **AKG D3500**

TYPE: **dynamic**

PICKUP PATTERN: **cardioid**

FREQUENCY RESPONSE: **60Hz-20kHz**

SENSITIVITY: **2.5mV/Pa**

NOISE: **22dBA**

MAXIMUM SPL: **156dB at 3% THD**

IMPEDANCE: **600 ohms**

BASS CUT (HIGHPASS FILTER): **yes**

ALSO AVAILABLE FROM AKG:

C5600 condenser instrument mic

MAKE AND MODEL: **Audio-Technica AT4041**

TYPE: **electret condenser**

PICKUP PATTERN: **cardioid**

FREQUENCY RESPONSE: **20Hz-20kHz**

SENSITIVITY: **-36dB (15.8mV) +/-2dB, re 1V/Pa**

DYNAMIC RANGE: **121dB, 1kHz at max SPL**

SIGNAL-TO-NOISE RATIO: **70dB, 1kHz at 1 Pa**

MAXIMUM SPL: **145dB SPL, 1kHz at 1% THD**

IMPEDANCE: **100 ohms**

BASS CUT: **-12dB/octave at 80Hz**

LEGEND ——— 12° or more on axis (flat)
- - - - - Roll-off

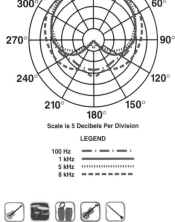

Scale is 5 Decibels Per Division

LEGEND

100 Hz	— · — · — · —
1 kHz	————
5 kHz	··················
8 kHz	- - - - - - - - -

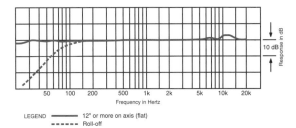

MAKE AND MODEL: **Audio-Technica ATM33a**

TYPE: **electret condenser**

PICKUP PATTERN: **cardioid**

FREQUENCY RESPONSE: **30Hz-20kHz**

SENSITIVITY: **-44dB (6.3mV), re 1V/Pa**

DYNAMIC RANGE: **113dB, 1kHz at max SPL**

SIGNAL-TO-NOISE RATIO: **70dB, 1kHz at 1 Pa**

MAXIMUM SPL: **137dB, 1kHz at 1% THD**

IMPEDANCE: **200 ohms**

FEATURES: **internal battery or phantom operation**

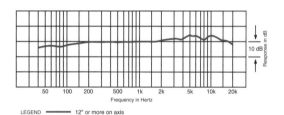

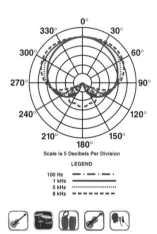

MAKE AND MODEL: **Audio-Technica ATM63HE**

TYPE: **dynamic**

PICKUP PATTERN: **hypercardioid**

FREQUENCY RESPONSE: **50Hz-18kHz**

SENSITIVITY: **-52dB (2.5 mV), re 1V/Pa**

IMPEDANCE: **600 ohms**

ALSO AVAILABLE FROM AUDIO-TECHNICA:

Pro 37R condenser mic

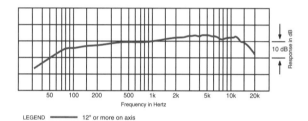

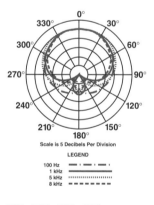

MAKE AND MODEL: **Audix D1/D2**

TYPE: **dynamic**

PICKUP PATTERN: **hypercardioid**

FREQUENCY RESPONSE: **38Hz-21kHz**

SENSITIVITY: **-71.5dB**

MAXIMUM SPL: **144dB**

IMPEDANCE: **250 ohms**

ALSO AVAILABLE FROM AUDIX: **D3 dynamic instrument mic**

MAKE AND MODEL: **Audix D4**

TYPE: **dynamic**

PICKUP PATTERN: **hypercardioid**

FREQUENCY RESPONSE: **30Hz-18kHz**

SENSITIVITY: **-72dB**

MAXIMUM SPL: **144dB**

IMPEDANCE: **200 ohms**

FEATURES: **response tailored for low frequencies**

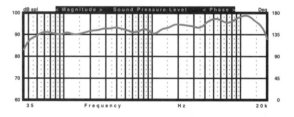

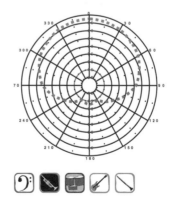

MAKE AND MODEL: **Audix OM-3xb**

TYPE: **dynamic**

PICKUP PATTERN: **hypercardioid**

FREQUENCY RESPONSE: **38Hz-21kHz**

SENSITIVITY: **-71.5dB**

MAXIMUM SPL: **144dB**

IMPEDANCE: **250 ohms**

ALSO AVAILABLE FROM AUDIX:

OM-5, OM-6 and OM-7 dynamic mics

MAKE AND MODEL: **Beyerdynamic M88**

TYPE: **dynamic**

PICKUP PATTERN: **hypercardioid**

FREQUENCY RESPONSE: **30Hz-20kHz**

SENSITIVITY: **-53dBV at 1kHz (open circuit, 0dB = 1V/Pa)**

IMPEDANCE: **200 ohms**

ALSO AVAILABLE FROM BEYERDYNAMIC:

M69 TG dynamic mic

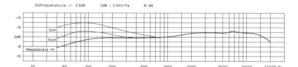

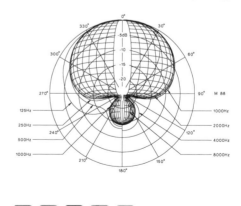

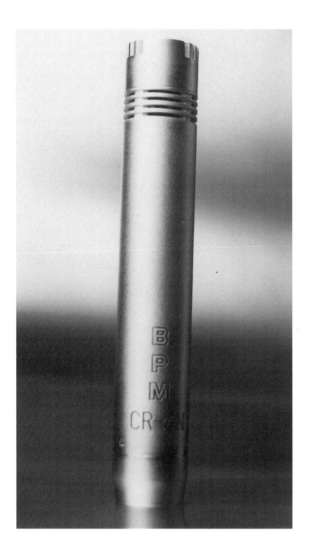

MAKE AND MODEL: **CAD/Equitek 88**
TYPE: **dynamic**
PICKUP PATTERN: **cardioid**
FREQUENCY RESPONSE: **40Hz-16kHz**
SENSITIVITY: **-75dB (ref 0dB = 1V/mbar)
at 1kHz, re 2mV/Pa**
IMPEDANCE: **150 ohms**
ALSO AVAILABLE FROM CAD/EQUITEK:
model 89, 28, 27 dynamic mics

MAKE AND MODEL: **BPM Studio Technik CR-4N card**
TYPE: **condenser**
PICKUP PATTERN: **cardioid**
FREQUENCY RESPONSE: **30Hz-20kHz**
SENSITIVITY: **12mV/Pa**
NOISE: **25dBA**
MAXIMUM SPL: **126dB, 1kHz at 0.5% THD**
IMPEDANCE: **200 ohms**
ALSO AVAILABLE FROM BPM:
CR-4N omnidirectional condenser mic

MAKE AND MODEL: **CAD/Equitek 95**

TYPE: **electret condenser**

PICKUP PATTERN: **cardioid**

FREQUENCY RESPONSE: **40Hz-20kHz**

SENSITIVITY:

-68dB (ref 0dB = 1V/mbar) at 1kHz, re 4mV/Pa

SIGNAL-TO-NOISE RATIO: **>55dB at 1 microbar**

MAXIMUM SPL: **130dB at 1% THD, open circuit**

IMPEDANCE: **150 ohms**

MAKE AND MODEL: **CAD/Equitek E-100**

TYPE: **condenser**

PICKUP PATTERN: **supercardioid**

FREQUENCY RESPONSE: **10Hz-18kHz**

SENSITIVITY: **17.8 mV/Pa at 1kHz**

SELF-NOISE: **16dBA SPL**

DYNAMIC RANGE: **132dB**

MAXIMUM SPL: **148dB w/pad**

IMPEDANCE: **200 ohms balanced**

PAD: **20dB**

BASS CUT (HIGHPASS FILTER): **yes**

MAKE AND MODEL: **Crown CM-200a**

TYPE: **electret condenser**

PICKUP PATTERN: **cardioid**

FREQUENCY RESPONSE: **80Hz-15kHz**

SENSITIVITY: **-53dBV/Pa, re 1V/Pa, 2.2mV**

SELF-NOISE: **21.5dBA**

SIGNAL-TO-NOISE RATIO: **72.5dB at 94dB SPL**

MAXIMUM SPL: **151dB at 3%THD**

IMPEDANCE: **200 ohms**

ALSO AVAILABLE FROM CROWN: **CM-310A dynamic mic**

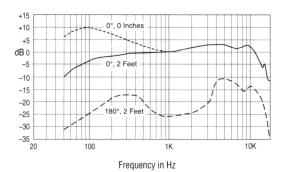

Frequency in Hz

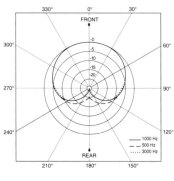

MAKE AND MODEL: **Crown CM-700**

TYPE: **condenser**

PICKUP PATTERN: **cardioid**

FREQUENCY RESPONSE: **30Hz-20kHz**

SENSITIVITY: **-52dB (2.5mV), re 1V/Pa**

NOISE: **21dBA SPL**

SIGNAL-TO-NOISE RATIO: **73dB at 94dB SPL**

MAXIMUM SPL: **151dB at 3% THD**

IMPEDANCE: **190 ohms**

BASS CUT (HIGHPASS FILTER): **2 positions**

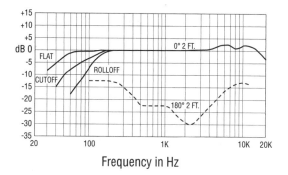

Frequency in Hz

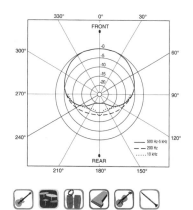

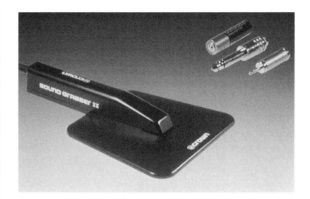

MAKE AND MODEL: **Crown PZM-30D**

TYPE: **boundary**

ELEMENT: **electret condenser**

PICKUP PATTERN: **hemispherical**

FREQUENCY RESPONSE: **20Hz-20kHz**

SENSITIVITY: **7mV/Pa (open-circuit)**

SELF-NOISE: **20dBA**

SIGNAL-TO-NOISE RATIO: **74dB at 94dB SPL**

MAXIMUM SPL: **150dB at 3% THD**

IMPEDANCE: **240 ohms**

ALSO AVAILABLE FROM CROWN: **PZM-6D boundary mic**

MAKE AND MODEL: **Crown Sound Grabber II**

TYPE: **boundary**

ELEMENT: **electret condenser**

PICKUP PATTERN: **hemispherical**

FREQUENCY RESPONSE: **50Hz-16kHz**

SENSITIVITY: **20mV/Pa (-54dBV/Pa)**

IMPEDANCE: **1,600 ohms, unbalanced**

ALSO AVAILABLE FROM CROWN: **PZM-185 boundary mic**

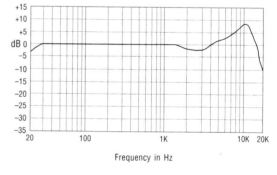

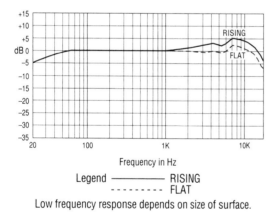

Frequency in Hz

Legend ————— RISING

- - - - - - - - - FLAT

Low frequency response depends on size of surface.

MAKE AND MODEL: **Earthworks TC30K**

TYPE: **condenser**

PICKUP PATTERN: **omnidirectional**

FREQUENCY RESPONSE:

9Hz-25kHz +/-1dB, 9Hz-30kHz +1/-3dB

SENSITIVITY: **8mV/Pa (-42dBV/Pa)**

NOISE: **27dBA**

MAXIMUM SPL: **151dB w/5k ohm load**

IMPEDANCE: **600 ohms**

MAKE AND MODEL: **Electro-Voice N/D 308B**

TYPE: **dynamic**

PICKUP PATTERN: **cardioid**

FREQUENCY RESPONSE: **50Hz-20kHz**

SENSITIVITY: **-53dB at 1kHz**

DYNAMIC RANGE: **141dB**

IMPEDANCE: **150 ohms**

ALSO AVAILABLE FROM EV:

N/D 408B dynamic instrument mic

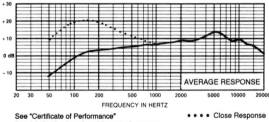

See "Certificate of Performance"
(provided with microphone) for actual response

• • • • Close Response

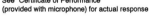

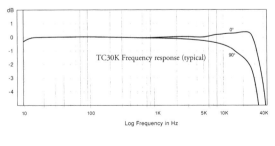

TC30K Frequency response (typical)

MAKE AND MODEL:

Electro-Voice RE200

TYPE: **condenser**

PICKUP PATTERN: **cardioid**

FREQUENCY RESPONSE:

50Hz-18kHz

SENSITIVITY: **10mV/Pa**

NOISE: **21dBA**

DYNAMIC RANGE: **109dB**

IMPEDANCE: **200 ohms**

MAKE AND MODEL: **Peavey PVM 357**

TYPE: **electret condenser**

PICKUP PATTERN: **cardioid**

FREQUENCY RESPONSE: **50Hz-16kHz**

SENSITIVITY: **-67dB (open circuit, with EQ/output module)**

MAXIMUM SPL: **148dB at 1% THD**

IMPEDANCE: **600 ohms**

FEATURES: **EQ/preamp module**

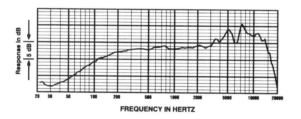

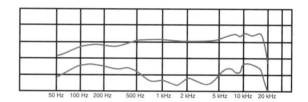

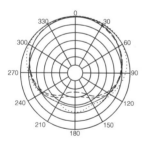

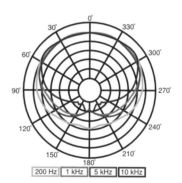

MAKE AND MODEL: **Peavey PVM 520i**

TYPE: **dynamic**

PICKUP PATTERN: **cardioid**

FREQUENCY RESPONSE: **45Hz-19kHz**

SENSITIVITY: **-52dB (0dB = 1mW/Pa)**

IMPEDANCE: **400 ohms**

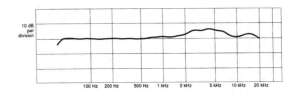

MAKE AND MODEL: **Peavey PVM 480**

TYPE: **electret condenser**

PICKUP PATTERN: **supercardioid**

FREQUENCY RESPONSE: **40Hz-20kHz**

SENSITIVITY: **-64dB (open circuit,
0dB = 1 volt/dyne/cm²)**

SIGNAL-TO-NOISE RATIO: **>69dB ref 1Pa**

MAXIMUM SPL: **128dB**

IMPEDANCE: **500 ohms**

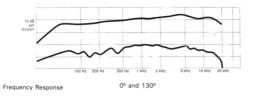

Frequency Response   0° and 130°

MAKE AND MODEL: **Sennheiser MD421II**
TYPE: **dynamic**
PICKUP PATTERN: **cardioid**
FREQUENCY RESPONSE: **30Hz-17kHz**
SENSITIVITY: **2mV/Pa (+/-2.5dB)**
IMPEDANCE: **200 ohms**
BASS CUT (HIGHPASS FILTER): **5 positions**
ALSO AVAILABLE FROM SENNHEISER:

MD 441U dynamic mic

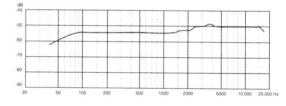

MAKE AND MODEL: **RØDE NT1**
TYPE: **condenser**
PICKUP PATTERN: **cardioid**
FREQUENCY RESPONSE: **20Hz-20kHz**
SENSITIVITY: **18mV/Pa**
SELF-NOISE: **17dBA**
MAXIMUM SPL: **135dB**
IMPEDANCE: **200 ohms**

MAKE AND MODEL: **Sennheiser MD504**

TYPE: **dynamic**

PICKUP PATTERN: **cardioid**

FREQUENCY RESPONSE: **40Hz-18kHz**

SENSITIVITY: **1.8mV/Pa**

MAXIMUM SPL: **>160dB**

IMPEDANCE: **350 ohms**

MAKE AND MODEL: **Sennheiser ME64/K6**

TYPE: **condenser**

FREQUENCY RESPONSE: **40Hz-20kHz (+/-2.5dB)**

SENSITIVITY: **31mV/Pa (+/-2.5dB)**

NOISE: **16dBA**

MAXIMUM SPL: **130dB at 1kHz**

IMPEDANCE: **200 ohms**

BASS CUT (HIGHPASS FILTER): **200Hz**

ALSO AVAILABLE FROM SENNHEISER:

ME62 omnidirectional mic head

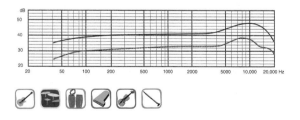

MAKE AND MODEL: **Shure SM57**
TYPE: **dynamic**
PICKUP PATTERN: **cardioid**
FREQUENCY RESPONSE:
40Hz-15kHz
SENSITIVITY: **-75.5dB (0.17mV)**
IMPEDANCE: **150 ohms**

MAKE AND MODEL: **Shure Beta 57A**
TYPE: **dynamic**
PICKUP PATTERN: **supercardioid**
FREQUENCY RESPONSE: **50Hz-16kHz**
SENSITIVITY: **-71dB (0.28mV open circuit)**
IMPEDANCE: **150 ohms**
ALSO AVAILABLE FROM SHURE BROS:
**Beta 56 instrument dynamic mic,
Beta 52 bass drum dynamic mic**

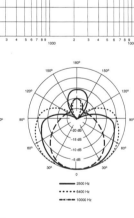

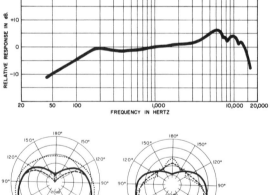

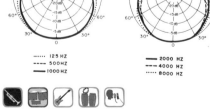

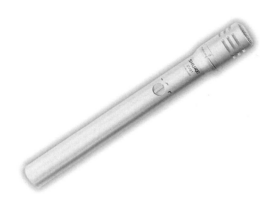

MAKE AND MODEL: **Shure SM81**

TYPE: **condenser**

PICKUP PATTERN: **cardioid**

FREQUENCY RESPONSE: **20Hz-20kHz**

SENSITIVITY: **-65dB (0.56mV open circuit)**

SELF-NOISE: **16dBA**

SIGNAL-TO-NOISE RATIO: **78dB**

MAXIMUM SPL: **136dB (146dB w/pad)**

IMPEDANCE: **150 ohms**

PAD: **-10dB**

BASS CUT (HIGHPASS FILTER):

-6dB/octave at 100Hz, -18dB/octave at 80Hz

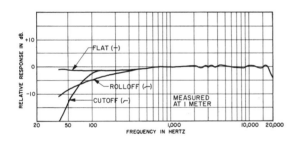

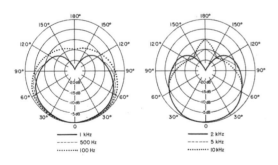

MAKE AND MODEL: **Shure SM94**

TYPE: **electret condenser**

PICKUP PATTERN: **cardioid**

FREQUENCY RESPONSE: **40Hz-16kHz**

SENSITIVITY: **-69dB (0.35mV)**

SELF-NOISE: **22dBA**

DYNAMIC RANGE: **119dB**

MAXIMUM SPL: **141dB (800 ohm load)**

IMPEDANCE: **150 ohms**

FEATURES: **battery or phantom power operation**

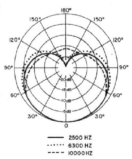

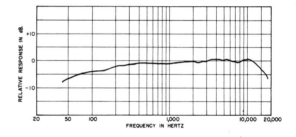

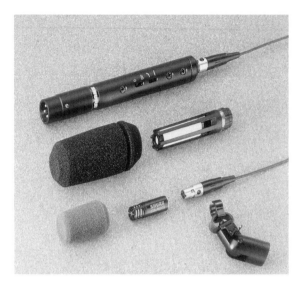

MAKE AND MODEL: **Shure SM98A**

TYPE: **electret condenser**

PICKUP PATTERN: **cardioid**

FREQUENCY RESPONSE: **40Hz-20kHz**

SENSITIVITY: **-80dB (0.10mV)**

EQUIVALENT INPUT NOISE: **34dBA**

DYNAMIC RANGE: **121dB**

SIGNAL-TO-NOISE RATIO: **60dB at 94dB SPL**

MAXIMUM SPL: **155dB (800 ohm load)**

IMPEDANCE: **150 ohms**

BASS CUT (HIGHPASS FILTER): **-12dB/octave at 80Hz**

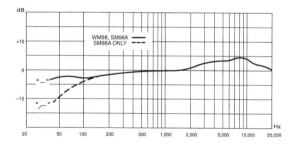

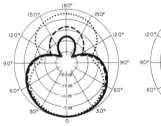

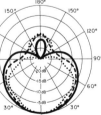

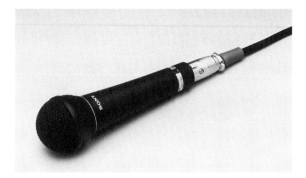

MAKE AND MODEL: **Sony F-740**

TYPE: **dynamic**

PICKUP PATTERN: **cardioid**

FREQUENCY RESPONSE: **50Hz-18kHz**

SENSITIVITY: **-54B +/-2dB (0dB = 1V/Pa at 1kHz)**

IMPEDANCE: **400 ohms**

ALSO AVAILABLE FROM SONY:

F-710, F-720, F-730, F-780 dynamic mics

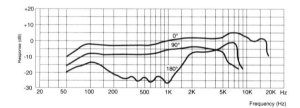

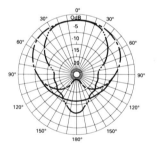

MAKE AND MODEL: **Stedman N90**

TYPE: **dynamic**

PICKUP PATTERN: **cardioid**

FREQUENCY RESPONSE: **35Hz-19kHz**

SENSITIVITY: **-57dB**

MAXIMUM SPL: **>155dB**

IMPEDANCE: **250 ohms**

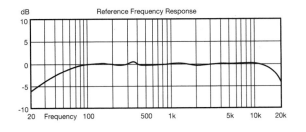

CHAPTER 28

Microphones From $500 to $1,000

| Acoustic Guitar | Bass Instruments | Brass | Cymbals | Drums | Electric Guitar | Percussion | Piano | Strings | Vocals | Woodwinds |

MAKE AND MODEL:

AKG C3000

TYPE: **condenser**

PICKUP PATTERN:

cardioid, hypercardioid

FREQUENCY RESPONSE:

20Hz-20kHz

SENSITIVITY:

20mV/Pa (cardioid)

NOISE: **18.5dBA**

MAXIMUM SPL:

137dB at 0.5% THD

IMPEDANCE: **200 ohms**

PAD: **-10dB**

BASS CUT (HIGHPASS FILTER):

12dB/octave at 75Hz or 150Hz

Author's Pick

MAKE AND MODEL:

Audio-Technica AT4033/SM

TYPE: **electret condenser**

PICKUP PATTERN: **cardioid**

FREQUENCY RESPONSE: **30Hz-20kHz**

SENSITIVITY: **-32dB (25.1mV) +/-2dB, re 1V/1Pa**

SELF-NOISE: **17dBA**

DYNAMIC RANGE:

128dB, 1kHz at max SPL

SIGNAL-TO-NOISE RATIO:

77dB, 1kHz at 1 Pa

MAXIMUM SPL: **145dB SPL, 1kHz at 1% THD 155dB SPL w/10dB pad**

IMPEDANCE: **100 ohms**

PAD: **10dB**

BASS CUT (HIGHPASS FILTER): **80Hz, 12dB/octave**

ALSO AVAILABLE FROM AUDIO-TECHNICA:

AT4051 condenser mic

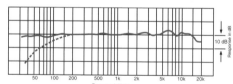

LEGEND ——— 12" or more on axis (flat)
------- Hi-pass

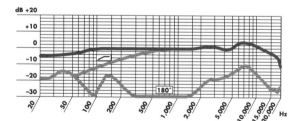

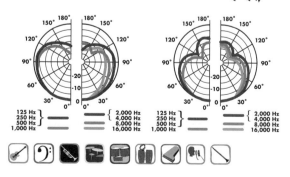

| 125 Hz | 250 Hz | 500 Hz | 1,000 Hz | { 2,000 Hz | 4,000 Hz | 8,000 Hz | 16,000 Hz |

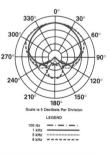

Scale is 5 Decibels Per Division

LEGEND
100 Hz
1 kHz
5 kHz
8 kHz

MAKE AND MODEL: **Audio-Technica AT4050**

TYPE: **condenser**

PICKUP PATTERN: **omnidirectional, cardioid, bidirectional**

FREQUENCY RESPONSE: **20Hz-20kHz**

SENSITIVITY: **-36dB (15.8 mV) +/-2dB, re 1V/1 Pa**

SELF-NOISE: **17dBA**

DYNAMIC RANGE: **132dB, 1kHz at max SPL**

SIGNAL-TO-NOISE RATIO: **77dB, 1kHz at 1 Pa**

MAXIMUM SPL: **149dB SPL, 1kHz at 1% THD; 159dB SPL, w/10dB pad**

IMPEDANCE: **100 ohms**

PAD: **10dB**

BASS CUT (HIGHPASS FILTER): **80Hz, 12dB/octave**

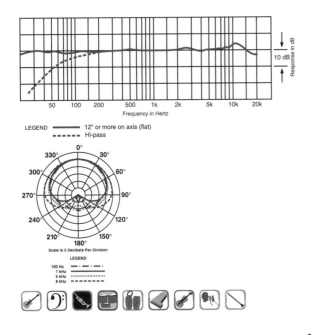

MAKE AND MODEL: **Audix SCX-one**

TYPE: **condenser**

PICKUP PATTERN: **cardioid**

FREQUENCY RESPONSE: **40Hz-20kHz**

SENSITIVITY: **14mV/Pa**

MAXIMUM SPL: **130dB**

OTHER CAPSULES: **omnidirectional, omnidirectional with presence peak, hypercardioid, -10dB pad**

MAKE AND MODEL: **BPM Studio Technik CR-73 II**

TYPE: **condenser**

PICKUP PATTERN: **omnidirectional, cardioid**

FREQUENCY RESPONSE: **40Hz-18kHz**

SENSITIVITY: **12mV/Pa**

NOISE: **26dBA**

MAXIMUM SPL: **124dB (1kHz at 0.5% THD)**

IMPEDANCE: **200 ohms**

PAD: **-10dB**

BASS CUT (HIGHPASS FILTER): **-10dB at 80Hz**

ALSO AVAILABLE FROM BPM: **CR-73 condenser mic**

MAKE AND MODEL: **Beyerdynamic M160**

TYPE: **dual dynamic ribbon**

PICKUP PATTERN: **hypercardioid**

FREQUENCY RESPONSE: **40Hz-18kHz**

IMPEDANCE: **200 ohms**

ALSO AVAILABLE FROM BEYERDYNAMIC:

M260 hypercardioid ribbon mic

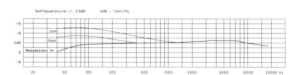

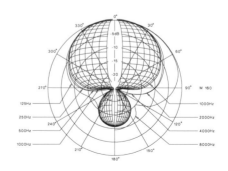

MAKE AND MODEL: **CAD/Equitek E-300**

TYPE: **condenser**

PICKUP PATTERN:

omnidirectional, cardioid, bidirectional

FREQUENCY RESPONSE: **10Hz-20kHz**

NOISE: **11dBA**

DYNAMIC RANGE: **137dB**

SIGNAL-TO-NOISE RATIO: **83dB (at 94dB SPL)**

MAXIMUM SPL: **148dB w/pad**

IMPEDANCE: **200 ohms**

PAD: **-20dB**

BASS CUT (HIGHPASS FILTER): **80Hz**

FEATURES: **internal extended-headroom battery power supply**

ALSO AVAILABLE FROM CAD/EQUITEK:

E200 multi-pattern condenser mic

MAKE AND MODEL:

Earthworks TC40K

TYPE: **condenser**

PICKUP PATTERN: **omnidirectional**

FREQUENCY RESPONSE: **9Hz-30kHz +/-1dB, 9Hz-40kHz +/-2dB**

SENSITIVITY: **8mV/Pa (-42dBV/Pa)**

NOISE: **26dBA**

MAXIMUM SPL:

150dB SPL w/5k ohm load

IMPEDANCE: **600 ohms**

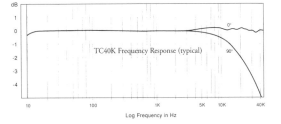

TC40K Frequency Response (typical)

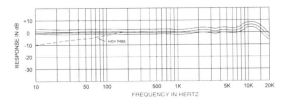

MAKE AND MODEL: **Electro-Voice RE1000**

TYPE: **condenser**

PICKUP PATTERN: **supercardioid**

FREQUENCY RESPONSE: **70Hz-18kHz**

SENSITIVITY: **11mV/Pa**

NOISE: **<14dBA**

MAXIMUM SPL: **130dB (1kHz at 1%)**

IMPEDANCE: **250 ohms**

BASS CUT (HIGHPASS FILTER): **130Hz**

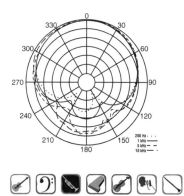

MAKE AND MODEL: **Electro-Voice RE20**

TYPE: **dynamic**

PICKUP PATTERN: **cardioid**

FREQUENCY RESPONSE: **45Hz-18kHz**

SENSITIVITY: **1.5mV/Pa at 1kHz**

IMPEDANCE: **50, 150 or 250 ohms**

BASS CUT (HIGHPASS FILTER): **yes**

ALSO AVAILABLE FROM EV: **PL20 dynamic instrument mic, RE27N/D dynamic instrument mic**

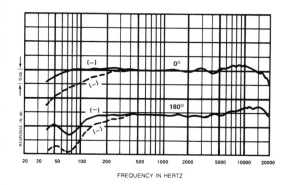

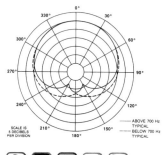

MAKE AND MODEL: **Electro-Voice RE38N/D**

TYPE: **dynamic**

PICKUP PATTERN: **cardioid**

FREQUENCY RESPONSE: **25Hz-20kHz**

SENSITIVITY: **-53dB at 1kHz**

IMPEDANCE: **150 ohms**

FEATURES: **16-position EQ selector**

MAKE AND MODEL: **Groove Tubes MD5SC**

TYPE: **condenser**

PICKUP PATTERN: **cardioid**

FREQUENCY RESPONSE: **20Hz-18kHz (+/-1.5dB)**

SENSITIVITY: **32mV/Pa**

NOISE: **22dBA**

MAXIMUM SPL: **134dB (144dB w/10dB pad)**

IMPEDANCE: **200 ohms**

PAD: **-10dB**

BASS CUT: **yes**

ALSO AVAILABLE FROM GROOVE TUBES:

MD5SM multi-pattern condenser mic

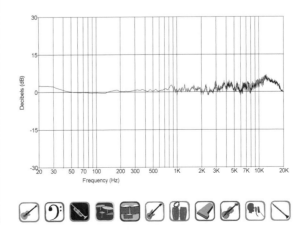

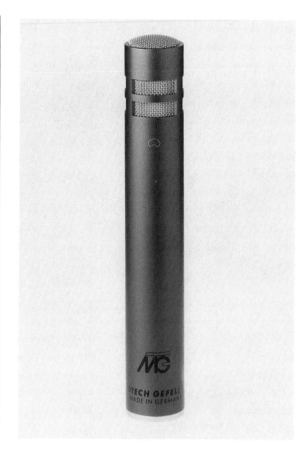

MAKE AND MODEL: **Langevin CR-3A**

TYPE: **condenser**

PICKUP PATTERN: **cardioid**

FREQUENCY RESPONSE: **40Hz-16kHz**

SIGNAL-TO-NOISE RATIO: **67dB (ref. level 1Pa)**

MAXIMUM SPL: **122dB, 25Pa at 1kHz at 0.5% THD**
132dB, 79Pa at 1kHz w/10dB pad

IMPEDANCE: **200 ohms**

PAD: **-10dB**

BASS CUT: **-6dB/octave at 100Hz**

MAKE AND MODEL: **Microtech Gefell M 300**

TYPE: **condenser**

PICKUP PATTERN: **cardioid**

FREQUENCY RESPONSE: **40Hz-18kHz**

SENSITIVITY: **12mV/Pa at 1kHz**

NOISE: **16dBA**

DYNAMIC RANGE: **119dB**

SIGNAL-TO-NOISE RATIO: **78dBA**

MAXIMUM SPL: **135dB THD <0.5%**

IMPEDANCE: **150 ohms**

ALSO AVAILABLE FROM MICROTECH GEFELL:

M 200-series and M 294-series condenser mics

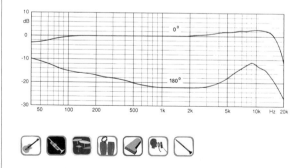

MAKE AND MODEL: **Microtech Gefell M 900**

TYPE: **condenser**

PICKUP PATTERN: **cardioid**

FREQUENCY RESPONSE: **40Hz-18kHz**

SENSITIVITY: **17mV/Pa**

NOISE: **13dBA**

DYNAMIC RANGE: **120dB**

SIGNAL-TO-NOISE RATIO: **81dBA**

MAXIMUM SPL: **133dB < 0.5% w/pad**

IMPEDANCE: **150 ohms**

PAD: **10dB**

BASS CUT (HIGHPASS FILTER): **-10dB at 90Hz**

ALSO AVAILABLE FROM MICROTECH GEFELL:

M 910 condenser mic

MAKE AND MODEL: **Microtech Gefell MT 711S**

TYPE: **condenser**

PICKUP PATTERN: **cardioid**

FREQUENCY RESPONSE: **40Hz-18kHz**

SENSITIVITY: **13mV/Pa**

NOISE: **14dBA**

DYNAMIC RANGE: **120dB**

MAXIMUM SPL: **134dB THD < 0.5%; 144dB w/pad**

IMPEDANCE: **150 ohms**

PAD: **10dB**

BASS CUT (HIGHPASS FILTER): **-10dB at 90Hz**

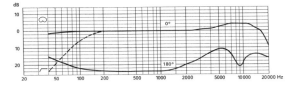

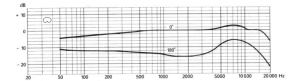

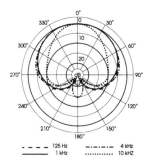

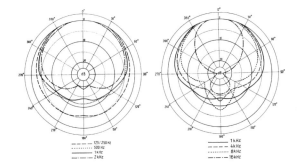

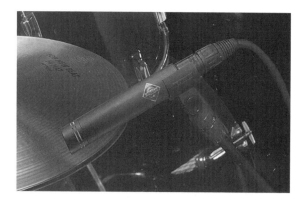

MAKE AND MODEL: **Neumann KM 184**

TYPE: **condenser**

PICKUP PATTERN: **cardioid**

FREQUENCY RESPONSE: **20Hz-20kHz**

SENSITIVITY: **15mV/Pa at 1kHz into 1k ohm**

NOISE: **16dBA**

DYNAMIC RANGE: **122dB**

SIGNAL-TO-NOISE RATIO: **78dB (DIN/IEC 651)**

MAXIMUM SPL: **138dB at 0.5% THD**

IMPEDANCE: **50 ohms**

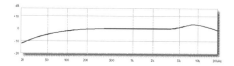

MAKE AND MODEL: **Neumann TLM-103**

TYPE: **condenser**

PICKUP PATTERN: **cardioid**

FREQUENCY RESPONSE: **20Hz-20kHz**

SENSITIVITY: **21mV/Pa at 1Hz into 1 Kohm**

NOISE: **7dBA**

DYNAMIC RANGE: **131dB**

SIGNAL-TO-NOISE RATIO: **87dB**

MAXIMUM SPL: **138dB**

IMPEDANCE: **50 ohms**

MAKE AND MODEL: **RØDE NT2**

TYPE: **condenser**

PICKUP PATTERN: **omnidirectional, cardioid**

FREQUENCY RESPONSE: **20Hz-20kHz**

SENSITIVITY: **16mV/Pa**

SELF-NOISE: **17dBA**

MAXIMUM SPL: **135dB; 145dB w/pad**

IMPEDANCE: **200 ohms**

PAD: **-10dB**

BASS CUT (HIGHPASS FILTER): **yes**

MAKE AND MODEL: **Sanken CU-31**

TYPE: **push-pull condenser**

PICKUP PATTERN: **cardioid**

FREQUENCY RESPONSE: **20Hz-18kHz**

SENSITIVITY: **3.5mV/Pa at 1kHz**

NOISE: **19dBA**

MAXIMUM SPL: **148dB, 1kHz at 1% THD**

IMPEDANCE: **200 ohms**

ALSO AVAILABLE FROM SANKEN:

CU-32 side-address condenser mic

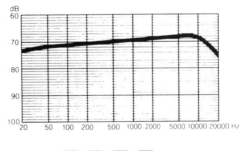

MAKE AND MODEL: **Stedman SC3**

TYPE: **condenser**

PICKUP PATTERN: **cardioid**

FREQUENCY RESPONSE: **25Hz-20kHz**

SENSITIVITY: **10mV/Pa**

NOISE: **13dBA**

SIGNAL-TO-NOISE RATIO: **81dB**

MAXIMUM SPL: **150dB**

IMPEDANCE: **250 ohms**

PAD: **-9dB, -18dB**

BASS CUT (HIGHPASS FILTER): **200Hz**

FEATURES: **high-frequency contour switch**

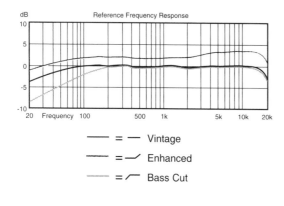

CHAPTER 29

Microphones From $1,000 to $1,500

Acoustic Guitar | Bass Instruments | Brass | Cymbals | Drums | Electric Guitar | Percussion | Piano | Strings | Vocals | Woodwinds

MAKE AND MODEL:
AKG C414B ULS
PICKUP PATTERN:
omnidirectional, cardioid, hypercardioid and bidirectional
FREQUENCY RESPONSE:
20Hz-20kHz
SENSITIVITY: **12.5mV/Pa**
NOISE: **14dBA**
MAXIMUM SPL:
140dB, 1kHz at 0.5%; 160dB w/pad
IMPEDANCE: **180 ohms**
PAD: **-10dB, -20dB**
BASS CUT (HIGHPASS FILTER):
12dB/octave at 75 Hz or 150 Hz

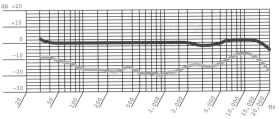

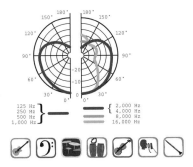

MAKE AND MODEL: **AKG Solidtube**
PICKUP PATTERN: **cardioid**
FREQUENCY RESPONSE: **20Hz-20kHz**
SENSITIVITY: **20mV/Pa**
SIGNAL-TO-NOISE RATIO: **74 dBA**
NOISE: **20 dBA**
MAXIMUM SPL: **130dB at 3% THD; 145dB w/pad**
IMPEDANCE: **200 ohms**
PAD: **-20db**
BASS CUT (HIGH-PASS FILTER): **12dB/octave at 100 Hz (on power supply)**
FEATURES: **tube electronics**

MAKE AND MODEL: **Beyerdynamic MC 834**
TYPE: **condenser**
PICKUP PATTERN: **cardioid**
FREQUENCY RESPONSE:
20Hz-20kHz
SENSITIVITY: **-34dBV at 1kHz (open circuit, 0dB = 1V/Pa)**
SIGNAL-TO-NOISE RATIO:
76dBA
MAXIMUM SPL:
130dB; 140dB or 150dB w/pad
IMPEDANCE: **180 ohms**
PAD: **-10dB, -20dB**
BASS CUT (HIGHPASS FILTER):
80Hz, 160Hz

MAKE AND MODEL: **BPM Studio Technik CR-95**
TYPE: **condenser**
PICKUP PATTERN: **omnidirectional, cardioid, bidirectional**
FREQUENCY RESPONSE: **20Hz-20kHz**
SENSITIVITY: **12mV/Pa**
SELF-NOISE: **16dBA**
MAXIMUM SPL: **148dB**
IMPEDANCE: **200 ohms**
PAD: **-10dB**
BASS CUT (HIGHPASS FILTER): **-6dB/octave at 150Hz**

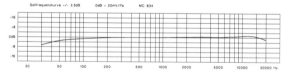

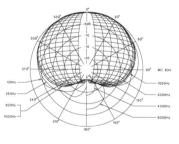

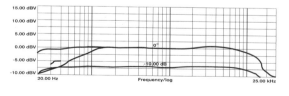

MAKE AND MODEL: **Coles 4038**
TYPE: **ribbon**
PICKUP PATTERN: **bidirectional**
FREQUENCY RESPONSE: **30Hz-15kHz**
SENSITIVITY: **-65dB (WRT 1V/Pa)**
MAXIMUM SPL: **125dB at 1% THD**
IMPEDANCE: **300 ohms**

MAKE AND MODEL: **Groove Tubes MD1a**
TYPE: **condenser**
PICKUP PATTERN: **cardioid**
FREQUENCY RESPONSE: **40Hz-18kHz (+/-4dB)**
SENSITIVITY: **50mV/Pa**
NOISE: **20dBA**
MAXIMUM SPL: **132dB**
IMPEDANCE: **50 ohms**
FEATURES: **tube electronics**

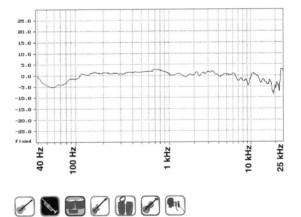

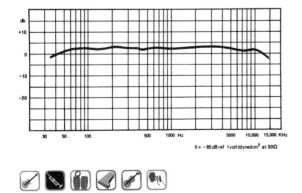

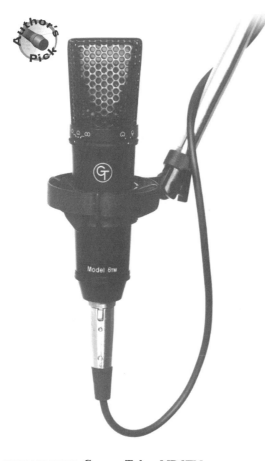

MAKE AND MODEL: **Groove Tubes MD6TM**

TYPE: **condenser**

PICKUP PATTERN: **omnidirectional, cardioid, supercardioid, bidirectional**

FREQUENCY RESPONSE: **20Hz-20kHz (+/-1.5dB)**

SENSITIVITY: **32mV/Pa**

NOISE: **23dBA**

MAXIMUM SPL: **130dB; 140dB w/10dB pad**

IMPEDANCE: **200 ohms**

PAD: **-10dB**

BASS CUT: **yes**

FEATURES: **tube electronics**

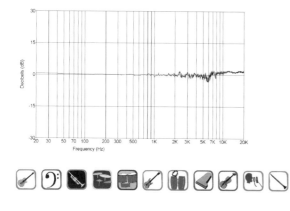

MAKE AND MODEL:

Lawson L47S

TYPE: **condenser**

PICKUP PATTERN: **cardioid**

FREQUENCY RESPONSE:

20Hz-20kHz

SENSITIVITY: **12.8mV/Pa**

(94dB SPL) at 1kHz

NOISE: **14dBA**

MAXIMUM SPL:

140dB SPL; 150dB w/pad

IMPEDANCE: **150 ohms**

PAD: **-10dB**

BASS CUT (HIGHPASS FILTER):

6dB/octave at 150Hz

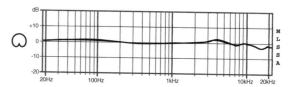

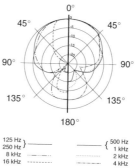

MAKE AND MODEL:
Microtech Gefell UMT 70 S

TYPE: **condenser**

PICKUP PATTERN: **omnidirectional, cardioid and bidirectional**

FREQUENCY RESPONSE:
40Hz-18kHz

SENSITIVITY: **7mV/Pa +/-3dB**

NOISE: **14dBA (IEC 651)**

DYNAMIC RANGE: **120dB**

SIGNAL-TO-NOISE RATIO: **80dBA**

MAXIMUM SPL:
139dB THD < 0.5%;
149dB w/10dB pad

IMPEDANCE: **150 ohms**

PAD: **10dB**

BASS CUT (HIGHPASS FILTER):
-10dB at 90Hz

MAKE AND MODEL: **Neumann TLM 193**

TYPE: **condenser**

PICKUP PATTERN: **cardioid**

FREQUENCY RESPONSE: **20Hz-20kHz**

SENSITIVITY: **11mV/Pa at 1kHz into 1 kohm**

NOISE: **10dBA**

DYNAMIC RANGE: **130dB**

SIGNAL-TO-NOISE RATIO: **84dB (DIN/IEC 651)**

MAXIMUM SPL: **140dB at 0.5% THD**

IMPEDANCE: **50 ohms**

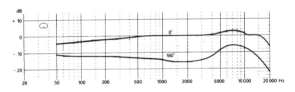

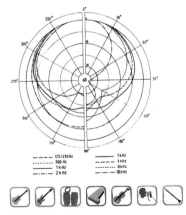

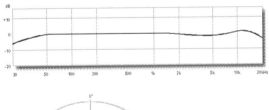

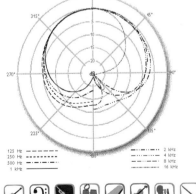

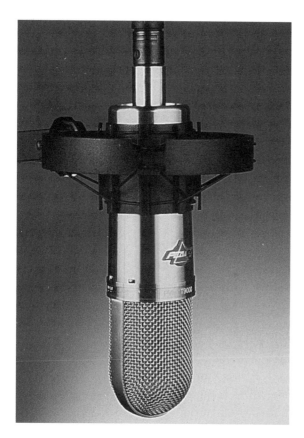

MAKE AND MODEL: **Peavey PVM T9000**

TYPE: **electret condenser**

PICKUP PATTERN: **cardioid**

FREQUENCY RESPONSE: **20Hz-20kHz**

SENSITIVITY: **-56dB (open circuit)**

MAXIMUM SPL: **137dB**

IMPEDANCE: **200 ohms**

PAD: **-10dB**

BASS CUT (HIGHPASS FILTER): **200Hz**

FEATURES: **tube electronics**

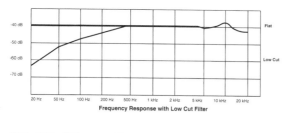

Frequency Response with Low Cut Filter

MAKE AND MODEL: **Sennheiser MKH40**

TYPE: **condenser**

PICKUP PATTERN: **cardioid**

FREQUENCY RESPONSE: **40Hz-20kHz (-3dB)**

SENSITIVITY: **25mV/Pa (8mV/Pa +/-1dB)**

NOISE: **12dBA**

MAXIMUM SPL: **134dB; 142dB w/pad**

PAD: **10dB**

IMPEDANCE: **150 ohms**

BASS CUT: **yes**

ALSO AVAILABLE FROM SENNHEISER:

MKH 20, MKH 30, MKH 50 condenser mics

MAKE AND MODEL: **Sony C-48**

TYPE: **condenser**

PICKUP PATTERN: **omnidirectional, cardioid, bidirectional**

FREQUENCY RESPONSE: **30Hz-16kHz**

SELF-NOISE: **less than 22dB SPL (0dB = 20uPa)**

DYNAMIC RANGE: **more than 106dB**

SIGNAL-TO-NOISE RATIO: **more than 72dB (A weighted at 1Pa)**

MAXIMUM SPL: **128dB SPL (0dB = 20uPa)**

IMPEDANCE: **150 ohms**

PAD: **10dB**

BASS CUT (HIGHPASS FILTER): **2 positions**

FEATURES: **internal battery or phantom power operation**

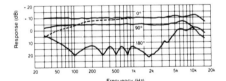

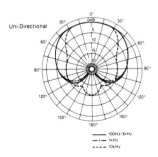

MAKE AND MODEL: **Soundelux U195**

TYPE: **condenser**

PICKUP PATTERN: **cardioid**

FREQUENCY RESPONSE: **20Hz-20kHz**

SENSITIVITY: **14mV/Pa**

SELF-NOISE: **12dBA**

DYNAMIC RANGE: **115dB**

SIGNAL-TO-NOISE RATIO: **82dBA**

MAXIMUM SPL: **125dB at 0.5% THD**

IMPEDANCE: **150 ohms**

PAD: **yes**

BASS CUT (HIGHPASS FILTER): **yes**

FEATURES: **switchable "fat" mode**

Microphone Sound Troubleshooter

Got a sound that's just not quite what it could be? Try these mic-related fixes before you reach for an electronic solution. If you can correct the problem before you roll tape (or spin a disc), your music will be better off in the long run.

PROBLEM	POSSIBLE SOLUTION
No sound at all	<u>Any mic</u> Replace cable Verify mixer channel correct <u>Condenser mic</u> Check phantom power Check battery OK
Sound too dark	Move directional mic back Try looser directional pattern Try different directional mic Try omnidirectional mic Place instrument on-axis with mic Place mic on-axis with instrument
Sound too bright	Move directional mic closer Try tighter directional pattern Try mic with flatter frequency response If condenser, try dynamic or ribbon mic Move instrument off-axis from mic Move mic off-axis from instrument
Vocal too sibilant	Rotate mic Move mic off-axis from mouth Move mic back Move mic above nose, point at mouth Try mic with flatter top-end response Try "slower" mic (especially dynamic or ribbon)

PROBLEM	POSSIBLE SOLUTION
Room sound (reverb) too loud	Verify mic pointed correctly Move mic closer Use tighter directional pattern Try different mic, same pattern Try different location in same room Try different room
Sound dry and sterile	Move mic back Try looser directional pattern Try omnidirectional mic Add room mic(s) Move instrument off-axis from mic
Levels inconsistent	Keep instrument stationary Try greater miking distance Attach mic directly to instrument
Sound distorted	Check mixer/recorder/preamp gain Move mic back from instrument Use mic with higher max SPL rating
Electronic noise (hiss) too loud	Move mic closer to instrument Use more sensitive mic Use mic with less self-noise
Loud pops from vocal	Use fabric pop filter Have vocalist sing "b" instead of "p" Have vocalist aim plosives away from mic Move mic back Move mic off-axis from mouth Use less-directional mic Use omnidirectional mic Try foam pop screen (last resort)
Too much bleed from other instruments	Move mic closer to instrument Use tighter directional pattern Aim directional mic's null at worst offender Move mic/instrument further from others
Sound lifeless	If using dynamic mic, try condenser mic Use mic with presence or treble boost Try different mic
Mic sound doesn't match acoustic sound	Try different mic position, same distance Try more distant mic position Try different mic
Uneven pickup of multiple instruments	Increase miking distance Use looser directional pattern Use omnidirectional mic Use both sides of bidirectional mic Place instruments closer together

The Home Studio Guide to Microphones

PROBLEM	POSSIBLE SOLUTION
Sound hollow	Single mic Move reflective surfaces (e.g., music stand) Move mic/instrument further from wall Move mic closer to instrument Try different mic position, same distance Multiple mics Move mics/instruments further from each other (observe 3:1 rule)
Constant rumble from mic	Check for nearby heating or air conditioning vent, move mic
Sound dull with long mic cable	Use only low-impedance mics
Mic picks up radio noises/buzzes	Use only balanced mics and cables

Microphone Manufacturers

AKG Acoustics
1449 Donelson Pike
Nashville, TN 37217
http://www.akg-acoustics.com

Audio-Technica
1221 Commerce Drive
Stow, OH 44224

Audix Corp.
9730 SW Hillman Court, Suite 620
Wilsonville, OR 97070
http://www.audixusa.com

BPM Studio Technik
7091 NW 51 Street
Miami, FL 33166
http://websamerica.com/bpmusa

Beyerdynamic
56 Central Avenue
Farmingdale, NY 11735

CAD/Equitek
PO Box 120
341 Harbor Street
Conneaut, OH 44030
http://www.ctiaudio.com

Coles Electroacoustics
(Distributed by Audio Engineering Associates)
1029 North Allen Avenue
Pasadena, CA 91104

Crown International
PO Box 1000
Elkhart, IN 46515
http://www.crownintl.com

Earthworks Inc.
PO Box 517
Wilton, NH 03086
http://www.earthwks.com

Electro-Voice
600 Cecil Street
Buchanan, MI 49107
http://www.eviaudio.com

Groove Tubes Audio
12866 Foothill Boulevard
Sylmar, CA 91342
http://www.groovetubes.com

Langevin
(Distributed by Manley Laboratories)
13880 Magnolia Avenue
Chino, CA 91710
http://www.manleylabs.com

Lawson Inc.
2741 Larmon Drive
Nashville, TN 37204
http://www.lawsonmicrophones.com

Microtech Gefell
(Distributed by G Prime Ltd.)
1790 Broadway, Fourth Floor
New York, NY 10019
http://www.gprime.com/mtg

Neumann USA
6 Vista Drive
PO Box 987
Old Lyme, CT 06371
http://www.neumannusa.com

Peavey Electronics Corp.
711 A Street
Meridian, MS 39301
http://www.peavey.com

RØDE Microphones
(Distributed by Event Electronics)
PO Box 4189
Santa Barbara, CA 93140
http://www.event1.com

Sanken Microphones
(Distributed by Audio Intervisual Design)
1155 La Brea Avenue
West Hollywood, CA 90038

Sennheiser Electronic Corp.
6 Vista Drive
Old Lyme, CT 06371
http://www.sennheiserusa.com

Shure Brothers Inc.
222 Hartrey Avenue
Evanston, IL 60202
http://www.shure.com

Sony Professional Audio
3 Paragon Drive
Montvale, NJ 07645
http://www.sony.com/proaudio

Soundelux
(Distributed by Group One Ltd.)
80 Sea Lane
Farmingdale, NY 11735

Stedman
4167 Stedman Drive
Richland, MI 49083
http://www.datawise.net/~webwld/sted/stedman.htm

Glossary

3:1 rule
To minimize phase cancellation, multiple mics should be spaced at least three times as far from each other as they are from their sound sources.

A-weighted
A noise measurement standard that takes into account the human ear's increased sensitivity to certain frequencies.

ambience
The natural reflections and reinforcement of sound in an enclosed space.

amplitude
The intensity of a sound wave or electrical signal.

anti-node
A place where a cyclical waveform (usually sound pressure) is at its lowest point. See also *node.*

attenuation
The amount of reduction in intensity of a sound or electrical signal.

attenuator
An electrical circuit that reduces the strength of an electrical signal. See also *pad.*

axial
A microphone design that places the element perpendicular to the body of the mic. Axial directional mics are most sensitive to sounds end-on. Also called "end-fire." See also *side-address.*

backplate
The disc (often perforated) that forms the rigid back surface of a condenser microphone.

balanced wiring
Carries a regular and phase-inverted version of the audio signal, which allows a mic preamp to cancel any noise picked up in the cable.

basket
See *suspension basket.*

bel
A logarithmic unit of measure for sound pressure level named after Alexander Graham Bell. See also *decibel.*

bidirectional
A microphone pickup pattern with two opposing lobes of high sensitivity. Also called "figure-8."

Blumlein
A coincident stereo miking technique that places two bidirectional mics close together, angling their pickup angles by 90 degrees.

boundary mic
A microphone that eliminates phase cancellation by measuring the air pressure changes between a small condenser diaphragm and a large boundary plate.

capacitance
An electrical phenomenon that occurs when two conductors sit in close proximity, separated by an insulator.

cardioid
A heart-shaped mic pickup pattern that has the highest sensitivity directly in front of the mic and the lowest directly behind it.

clipping
A distortion-inducing phenomenon that occurs when an electrical component is unable to reproduce the full voltage range of an electrical signal.

close-miking
A miking technique that places the mic (or mics) extremely close to an instrument, usually within a few inches.

coincident pair
Any stereo miking scheme that places the mic elements as close together as possible to eliminate time differences.

comb filter
A frequency response with a series of notches due to phase cancellation. So named because notches look like teeth on a comb.

compression
An area where sound has caused an increase in air pressure. See also *rarefaction*.

condenser
A rarely used synonym for "capacitor." Also a type of mic element that relies on capacitance to convert changes in air pressure (sound) to an electrical signal.

constructive interference
An area where direct and reflected sounds reinforce each other to create a higher sound pressure level at a given frequency.

contact mic
A microphone that senses the mechanical vibration of an instrument instead of sound.

cutoff frequency
The frequency above or below which an electronic filter begins attenuating signals.

damping
Acoustic material designed into a microphone to control resonances.

decibel
One tenth of a bel. Abbreviated "dB."

destructive interference
An area where direct and reflected sounds cancel each other out to create a reduced sound pressure level at a given frequency.

diaphragm
The part of a mic element that moves in response to changes in air pressure.

directional mic
A microphone that is more sensitive to sounds coming from certain directions.

distortion
Any unwanted alteration of (or deviation from) an electrical signal.

dynamic
A type of mic element that moves a coil of wire through a magnetic field to create a signal. Works like a loudspeaker in reverse.

dynamic range
The difference between the smallest and largest signals (or sounds) an electrical system can reproduce without distortion.

electret
A type of condenser element that has a permanent charge (usually in the backplate) and needs no external polarization voltage. See also *true condenser*.

element
The assembly that houses the mic diaphragm.

equivalent input noise
Correlates a mic's self-noise to a sound pressure level that would generate the same voltage.

field-effect transistor
A solid-state device used in most condenser mics to lower diaphragm impedance and provide gain to the signal. Abbreviated "FET."

flat
The characteristic of a mic that responds equally to all frequencies in the audible range.

frequency
A measurement of how many times an electrical signal or sound cycles from high to low in a second. Relates to human perception of pitch.

frequency response
Quantifies how a mic or other audio component captures or reproduces various frequencies.

fundamental
The lowest, strongest frequency contained in a given note. The fundamental defines the note's frequency and pitch. See also *overtone*.

gain
Electrical amplification, usually measured in dB.

handling noise
Quantifies how sensitive a microphone is to mechanical shocks and bumps. See also *suspension*.

headroom
The difference between the strength of an electrical signal and the point at which an electrical component begins clipping the signal.

hemispherical
A mic pickup pattern shaped like a sphere cut down the middle. Usually characteristic of the boundary microphone.

Hertz
A measurement of frequency equivalent to one cycle per second. Abbreviated "Hz."

hypercardioid
A mic pickup pattern tighter than a supercardioid at the front of the mic, but having an area of increased sensitivity directly behind the mic. See also *supercardioid*.

impedance
An electrical component's resistance to alternating current.

in phase
When the positive and negative excursions of two sound waves or electrical signals "line up" to reinforce one another. See also *out of phase*.

inductance
An electrical principle that causes electrons to flow when a wire passes through a magnetic field. Dynamic and ribbon mics rely on inductance to convert sound to an electrical signal.

interference tube
The long, perforated metal tube that gives the shotgun mic its highly directional pickup pattern.

inverse square rule
As sound moves away from its source, its intensity drops in proportion to the distance squared. A doubling of distance, for example, causes sound intensity to drop to one quarter.

maximum SPL
The loudest sound a mic can reproduce without severe distortion. Usually measured when a mic reaches 1% distortion in the output signal.

mic compression
The effect of a mic with slow transient response to "smooth out" the dynamics and transients of a sound.

mid-side
A coincident stereo miking setup that points a directional mic straight at the sound source and a bidirectional mic perpendicular to it. The two mic signals are converted to stereo through a simple mid-side decoder circuit. Usually abbreviated "M/S."

monophonic
A single audio signal or sound that conveys no localization information (a point source), usually abbreviated "mono." See also *stereo*.

multi-pattern mic
A microphone that uses electronic or mechanical means to provide numerous polar patterns from the same element.

near-coincident pair
A stereo miking technique that places two directional mics at an angle with some space between them. This stereo method captures both time and amplitude localization cues.

neodymium
A type of magnet that offers twice the strength per weight of traditional iron.

node
A place where a cyclical waveform (usually sound pressure) is at its highest point. See also *anti-node*.

noise
Any unwanted electrical or acoustical energy present in a signal or sound.

noise floor
The strength of a given mic's self-noise, usually expressed in dB.

NOS
A near-coincident stereo miking method that specifies a 90-degree deflection and 12-inch span between directional mics.

off-axis
Any sound entering a directional mic at an angle where the mic has reduced sensitivity. Also, any area not in-line with an instrument's high-frequency radiation pattern. Opposite of *on-axis*.

omnidirectional
A microphone pickup pattern that offers equal sensitivity to sounds coming from all directions.

on-axis
Any sound entering a directional mic at an angle where the mic has maximum sensitivity. Also, any area in-line with an instrument's high-frequency radiation pattern. Opposite of *off-axis*.

op-amp
Operational amplifier. A solid-state device designed to provide clean audio gain, used instead of an FET in some condenser mics.

ORTF technique
A near-coincident stereo miking method that specifies a 110-degree deflection and 7-inch span between directional mics.

out of phase
When the positive and negative excursions of two sound waves or electrical signals move in opposite directions to cancel one another. See also *in phase*.

overtone
A frequency emitted by an instrument that is higher than and mathematically related to the fundamental. Overtones help define an instrument's unique sonic character. See also *fundamental*.

pad
An electrical circuit that reduces the strength of an electrical signal. See also *attenuator*.

phantom power
A DC voltage (usually 48 volts) sent down the mic cable to power a condenser mic's internal electronics.

phase
Describes how two different waveforms (audio or electrical) relate to each other in time. See also *in phase, out of phase* and *phase cancellation*.

phase cancellation
The decrease in signal amplitude caused by the combination of two waveforms moving in opposite directions. When caused by a time delay, phase cancellation is most severe at specific, mathematically related frequencies.

polar chart
Shows a mic's sensitivity to sounds of specific frequencies coming from different directions.

preamp
An electrical device that boosts the level of a mic signal for recording or processing.

presence
A frequency band in the 2-5kHz region that conveys crispness and intelligibility in a sound.

pressure
A transducer system that exposes just one side of a diaphragm to air, making it sensitive to air pressure changes regardless of their direction. This creates an omnidirectional pickup pattern. See also *pressure gradient*.

pressure gradient
A transducer system that exposes both sides of a diaphragm to air, making it sensitive only to sounds that create a pressure difference (or gradient) between the two sides. This creates a bidirectional pickup pattern. See also *pressure*.

proximity effect
The tendency of a pressure-gradient mic to be more sensitive to low frequencies when placed close to the sound source. Amount of bass boost goes up as the mic moves closer to the sound source, starting at around two feet.

rarefaction
An area where sound has caused a decrease in air pressure. See also *compression*.

resonance
A band of frequencies at which an acoustic or electrical system stores energy. Resonance causes increased amplitude at and near the resonant frequency.

reverb
The smooth decay that results as a terminated sound continues to bounce around an enclosed space.

ribbon
An ultra-thin band of metal (sometimes less than one micron) used to sense sound in ribbon mics.

roll-off
The gradual attenuation of a signal above or below a certain frequency.

room mic
A mic placed to capture more ambient, reverberant sound than direct sound.

self-noise

The amount of noise a mic puts out even when no sound is present. Usually heard as hiss.

sensitivity

How strong a signal a microphone creates for a given sound pressure level.

shield

The braided wire or foil casing in an audio cable that keeps unwanted electromagnetic radiation from the signal-carrying conductor(s).

shotgun

A highly focused mic pickup pattern designed for distant pickup of sounds in a noisy or reverberant environment.

side-address

A mic design that places the element parallel to the mic body. Side-address directional mics are most sensitive to sounds coming from an angle perpendicular to the mic. Sometimes called "side-fire." See also *axial*.

signal-to-noise ratio

The difference between a mic's output at 94dB SPL and its noise floor, usually measured in dB. Abbreviated "S/N ratio."

sound pressure level

A measurement of the energy carried by a sound wave. Abbreviated "SPL."

spaced pair

A stereo miking method that places two mics (usually omnidirectional) several feet apart. Spaced pair miking captures arrival time differences, but no significant amplitude cues.

standing wave

An acoustic phenomenon where a low-frequency sound stays stationary between opposite walls in an enclosed space, reinforcing its amplitude.

stereo

A recording or reproduction system that captures or generates localization cues. Stereo sound creates a continuous soundfield between two speakers or headphones. See also *monophonic*.

supercardioid

A mic pickup pattern tighter than a cardioid at the front of the mic, but having an area of increased sensitivity directly behind the mic. See also *hypercardioid*.

suspension

The internal assembly designed to isolate a mic's element from mechanical shocks transmitted through the mic body. See also *handling noise*.

suspension basket

An external mount that attaches to a microphone stand, cradling the mic in elastic bands to isolate it from mechanical vibrations and shocks.

total harmonic distortion

A measurement of the amount of distortion an electrical component introduces to the signal. Usually abbreviated "THD."

transducer

Any device that converts one form of energy into another (e.g., sound into electricity).

transformer

A passive device that matches the impedance of two electrical circuits.

transient

An ultra-fast "spike" of sound often present at the very onset of a note, especially in percussion instruments.

transient response

The ability of a microphone to respond to very rapid changes in a sound.

transistor

A solid-state component that adds gain to an electrical signal.

true condenser

A condenser element design that requires polarization voltage from an external source. See also *electret*.

tube

A component that adds gain to an electrical signal. Tubes were the original electronic gain devices used for decades before the advent of the transistor.

voltage

An electrical characteristic that quantifies the potential for electron flow. Relating electricity to water flowing in a pipe, voltage is analogous to pressure.

wavelength

The distance between adjacent compressions or rarefactions of a sound, or how far sound travels in one complete cycle. Wavelength is inversely proportional to *frequency*.

X-Y

A stereo miking technique that places the elements of two directional mics as close as possible to each other, angling the patterns outward at roughly 90 degrees. This method captures amplitude differences, but no delay cues.

XLR connector

A locking, three-pin connector that usually carries a balanced audio signal.

Suggested Reading

There's a lot to learn about microphones, sound and recording techniques; and there are plenty of materials available to help. Here are a few resources to take you to the next level of knowledge about microphones.

Books

Bartlett, Bruce. *Stereo Microphone Techniques.* Boston/London: Focal Press, 1991

Borwick, John. *Microphones: Technology and Technique.* Boston/London: Focal Press, 1990

Gayford, Michael, Ed. *Microphone Engineering Handbook.* Boston/London: Focal Press, 1994

Huber, David and Runstein, Robert. *Modern Recording Techniques, 4th Edition.* Indianapolis, IN: Sams Publishing, 1995

Mellor, David. *Recording Techniques for Small Studios.* Kent, UK: PC Publishing, 1993

Nisbett, Alec. *The Use of Microphones, 4th Edition.* Boston/London: Focal Press, 1993

Magazines

Electronic Musician. 6400 Hollis Street, Suite 12, Emeryville, CA 94608; (510) 653-3307

Mix. 6400 Hollis Street, Suite 12, Emeryville, CA 94608; (510) 653-3307

Pro Audio Review. 5827 Columbia Pike, 3rd Floor, Falls Church, VA 22041; (703) 998-7600

Recording. 5412 Idylwild Trail, Suite 100, Boulder, CO 80301; (303) 516-9118

Multimedia

(CD-ROM)
Allen Sides Microphone Cabinet, Cardinal Business Media; (510) 653-3307

(Audio CD/Book)
Critical Listening and Auditory Perception by F. Alton Everest, MixBooks; (510) 653-3307

Other Resources

Shure Microphone Techniques for Music Sound Reinforcement, and *Shure Microphone Techniques for Music Recording;* Shure Brothers Inc.; (800) 25-SHURE

Crown Microphone Application Guide for Studio Recording, Crown Boundary Microphone Application Guide, and *Crown Microphone Application Guide: CM, LM and GLM Series;* Crown International; (219) 294-8000

Microphones for Professional and Semi-Professional Applications; Neumann USA; (860) 434-5220

Index

octave 3
off-axis placement 59
off-axis response 32, 44, 62, 78
off-axis sound 55
omnidirectional 21
omnidirectional mic 21, 52
ORTF 99
out of phase 4
overtones 3
pad 34, 46
pattern selector switch 27
perceived distance 58
percussion 75
phantom power 12, 38
phase 4
phase cancellation 5, 24, 55, 57, 63
piano 81
piccolo 88
pickup pattern 62
plosives 93
polar response chart 32
presence boost 45
pressure doubling 16
pressure system 21
pressure-gradient system 21, 24
proximity effect 21, 29, 32, 44, 52, 57, 62, 92
rental mics 110
resonance 41
reverberation 6
ribbon element 14
room mics 53, 55, 60
rotating speaker 83
ruggedness 38
saxophone 88
self-noise 19, 35, 47
sensitivity 34, 46, 47
shaker 75
shield 6
shock-mount basket 33
shotgun pattern 24
sibilance 92, 93
side-address 27, 48
signal-to-noise ratio 35
small-diaphragm condenser 14
snare drum 68
solo vocal 92
sonic fingerprint 42
sound pressure level 3
sound rejection 20
spaced pair 99
stereo 40
stereo effect 53
stereo mic 105
stereo miking 96, 103

Stereosonic 98
string ensemble 90
supercardioid mic 52
supercardioid pattern 23
talking drums 75
tambourine 75
temperature 14, 39
testing mics 110, 111
timbales 75
tom 68
transducer 9
transient 30
transient response 11, 13, 15, 17, 30, 38, 42
triangles 76
trombone 86
trumpet 86
tuba 86
tube mic 17
two-way mic 20
unbalanced signal 7
upright bass 90
upright piano 82
used mics 108
vibes 76
vintage mic 109
viola 90
violin 90
vocal ensemble 93
voice coil 10
wavelength 3, 20, 57
woodwinds 88
X-Y 98
XLR connector 7, 8
xylophone 76